Pet Dogs Democratic Party Manifesto

By

Alfie Dog

with a little help from

Rosemary J. Kind

Copyright © 2015 Alfie Dog and Rosemary J. Kind

All rights reserved. Any unauthorised broadcasting, public performance, copying or recording will constitute an infringement of copyright. No part of this book may be reproduced or transmitted in any form or by any means, electronically or mechanical, including photocopying, fax, data transmittal, internet site, recording or any information storage or retrieval system without the express written permission of the publisher except for the use of brief quotations in a book review.

Printed in the United Kingdom

First Printing, 2015 Alfie Dog Limited

The author can be found at: authors@alfiedog.com

Cover image: Katie Stewart www.magicowldesign.com

ISBN 978-1-909894-25-9

Published by
Alfie Dog Limited
Rose Bank, Norton Lindsey,
Warwickshire, CV35 8JQ
Tel: 07712 647754

DEDICATION

Elio & Anka
My beloved parents
Alfie

CONTENTS

Acknowledgments	i
Introduction	1
Our Policies	3
Education	4
Employment and Pensions	10
Foreign Policy and Defence	16
Immigration	21
Healthcare	26
Breeding	32
Crime and Punishment	43
Civil Liberties and Basic Canine Rights	49
Arts and Culture	66
Environment	70
Welfare	75
Economy and Taxation	77
Trade and Industry	83
Agriculture and Fishing	84
Transport	87
Animal Testing	92
Disability / Differing Ability	94
Church	96
Parliament	98
Housing and Planning	103
Europe	105
Conclusion	107
Author Profiles	108

ACKNOWLEDGMENTS

Sincere thanks to the wonderful Katie Stewart at Magic Owl Design for bringing my ideas to life in the illustrations. www.magicowldesign.com

Also to Sonja van den Durpel for her part in bringing Alfie into the world and allowing him to live with me. Not a day goes by that I am not grateful for this most precious gift.

INTRODUCTION

Being both a thinking dog and a dog of action, it occurred to me that the world would be a far better place if dogs were more involved in the political processes which shape our lives. It was a bit like knocking down a domino line, once I had that thought, the needs of dogs and the injustices we face became apparent one after another. That was what inspired me to form the Pet Dogs Democratic Party (PDDP) and which brings me to challenge dogs and humans everywhere to take up the cause and embrace the policies of our party.

Oh you may have thought that the idea of the PDDP running the country was a ridiculous one, but come on, be honest, do you really think a country run by dogs would be any more of a mess? Think of the upsides. You would be able to rely on plenty of naps, and eating, being very high on our list of priorities. It would no longer be socially unacceptable to have a good scratch in public and there would be a rapid end to the British reserve. Handshaking would be a thing of the past, with everyone being encouraged to have a good sniff of each other as a means of introduction. Doesn't seem such a stupid idea now, does it?

Unlike many other political parties you will not find the old 'class' distinctions holding sway. Mongrels, crossbreeds and pedigrees stand equal in our eyes, whether they be human or canine. We want a society which is about equality of opportunity for all, regardless of background. You don't have to be a dog to join the party any more than you have to be a Martian to join the Green party. It is all about signing up to our values and saying, 'Yes, I want a world in which a dog has equal rights. I want a world in which the civil liberties of a dog are upheld and valued. I want a world in which 4 legs and 2 legs stand equal, side by side in our struggle for a better world.'

If you have not already done so, in addition to reading our manifesto, you can buy membership of the party for yourself or as a gift for someone else (we charge extra if that someone is a C A T). You will receive a membership pack and have your name added to our list of party members. You can sign up at www.pddp.org.uk, where you will also find links to our party merchandise.

Working dogs are, of course, welcome to join, but we do believe that even working dogs should have a hearth to share in an evening and, besides which, the Pet and Working Dogs Democratic Party is a big of a mouthful, although when I think about it, PAW DDP is quite attractive as an acronym.

Be proud, say it loud, 'I am a member of the Pet Dogs Democratic Party!'

OUR POLICIES

We have endeavoured to present our policies in a coherent way on most areas. I know that literacy at this stage may be a problem, and many dogs will need to ask their humans to read this to them, better that than asking the cat! However, we do need to get our message out. How can dogs rise up and take control of their own destiny if they haven't thought of all the issues that they will face? Oh I admit, as with the recent debates on independence, there may be things we haven't fully thought through, but reading the manifestos of the other parties it seems to me we aren't alone in that and our economic claims are no more extravagant than anyone else's.

We don't have previous experience in power, but everyone has to start somewhere and let's be honest, if someone is going to get it wrong, it's far easier to take if they then look up at you with doleful brown eyes and nuzzle your leg in apology. Dogs of the world unite, although you may need a little help from your humans to stop the ensuing chaos!

I don't want to be one of those fake parties that buys its policies 'off the shelf', because there is only really one issue that the party knows anything about. I want to put something together that will stack up. I'm not absolutely sure I can see how the whole economic policy is going to work, but why should I worry about that when neither can any of the recent Governments?

EDUCATION

There can be few places more important to start than education.

Basic obedience training is not the same as education.
I decided to conduct a survey amongst other dogs, asking them about everything from what they were allowed to do at home to what they enjoyed doing in their spare time and what were their main concerns. I typed it all out on the computer and printed it out. When I started going round other dogs, asking them to write their answers to the questions, it turned out that many dogs can't actually read and write. I was shocked. Many had been to training schools, but despondently explained that all these had set out to do was teach them to obey rather than give them any of the tools they needed to be able to think for themselves. When you teach a dog to read you open up to him a whole new way of thinking and the ability to solve problems for himself. It is far more than just a useful skill. Teaching him to open the dog treat cupboard to help himself is a useful skill, teaching him to read gives him the tools he needs to start to redesign the dog treat cupboard for easier access.

It is no good letting humans take dogs in with their brainwashing. Dogs are thinking beings and can understand language as well as many of their humans, better in some cases. There are humans out there who say

PET DOGS DEMOCRATIC PARTY MANIFESTO

that dogs do not understand words, they just associate certain behaviours with particular sounds. Now I hate to be picky, but what is language if it isn't humans associating certain thoughts or behaviours with particular sounds? A French person associates the direction left with a different sound than a Russian person. Where I grew up in Belgium different parts of the country used different sounds even for these basic levels of communications. If it is ok to say a human can 'understand' words because of their sound why do people say that dogs don't understand? OK sure I can't string a whole sentence together and pronounce it in a way that you will recognise, but if you learnt to woof you would soon realise I am not limited to the odd word or two. It is time for humans to sit up and take notice of the underdog if you'll pardon the pun.

Bear in mind that English is our second language (woofing being our first) and even a good foreign speaker would only normally know 3000 to 5000 words in a second tongue. For those humans among you reading this, your dog doesn't seem so dumb now, does he? Just count up the number of words we understand and you'll soon start to realise what we're capable of if only we had the right education.

Maybe human adult education colleges should be running more courses in woofing. I don't mean so that we can learn economics from humans, but courses to teach humans to converse with us more effectively. Dr Dolittle wasn't strange. He was the normal one. It's the rest of the humans who are odd.

I wondered whether I should make it part of the PDDP manifesto that dogs shouldn't simply obey the commands of human beings. The subservience that it requires just does not become our species. We have brains. We can think for ourselves. We may think things like 'I wonder what his bottom smells like?' or 'Where will I find the nearest muck to roll in?' but we do think for ourselves. I suppose if we didn't have the brain we wouldn't be very good at learning all the commands. It would be a bit like trying to train your gerbil or goldfish to sit and stay, although even then, don't underestimate your gerbil!

What do we need to learn?

Why is it that humans think they have the monopoly on intelligent thinking? I get tucked up in bed at night with phrases like 'Enjoy dreaming of chasing rabbits'. What on earth makes humans think that our fine brains think of nothing deeper than rabbit chasing? It stands to reason that if humans can have a very wide range of intellect, so can dogs. Also in common with humans it may well be that the most intelligent of us dogs aren't the most practical or obedient. What level of original thought is involved in sitting on instruction?

We need to learn to read and write like everyone else. We need to learn to open the fridge door and how to use a can opener. We may need to adapt some gadgets specifically for paw use, but for that we will need inventors and scientists and crafts-dogs, just as humans need to learn a range of skills.

We are restricted to obedience training to keep is in a subservient position. It's time for that to change.

Adult Education

Remember it was a human who said 'you can't teach an old dog new tricks' not a dog. For the dogs among you, don't be cowed into thinking as you get past puppy classes that it is all over for you on an education front. You have your whole life ahead of you in which you can continue to learn new skills.

Education should be free to all pets
The first priority must be to have freely available education for all dogs regardless of their ability to pay for it. I'm not quite sure whether we are ready to make it compulsory, dogs have lived under the yoke of tyranny for too long and should not seek to replace it with a tyranny of our own making. However, an uneducated dog is ripe for human brainwashing and should be urged to set himself free through education.

What are we trying to achieve?
There is more to education than just learning to read and write. With education comes the freedom to make decisions for one's own life. With education comes the ability to achieve equality or at the very least equality of opportunity. With freedom comes responsibility and dogs must be ready to show there is more to us than chasing our tails and demonstrating that we can lick parts that humans only dream of reaching. We must rise to the challenge and play an active part in society.

In a recent survey 5 out of 8 dogs said they were not allowed on the sofa and 7 out of 8 were not allowed on the bed. It became clear quite early on in the survey that we were dealing with one very spoilt dog in the case of a certain Pekingese!

It was sad realising none of them were able to read books for themselves, although one or two of them said they shared in the bedtime stories that were read to the children in their houses. In response to being asked about their biggest concerns, I was depressed that these were so parochial. Not being able to open the dog biscuit cupboard came highest although on the whole they said they would rather open the fridge anyway. Of course these are important to a dog, but such trivialities should be everyday things as they are for humans, leaving us free to concentrate on the bigger issues. Not one of the dogs questioned talked about their lack of employment rights or the discrimination against dogs. It had never occurred to any of them that it was unreasonable for them to be left tied up outside the Post Office or that being refused entry to an airport was unfair. Without freely available education, covering a wide range of subjects, we can never achieve equality.

EMPLOYMENT & PENSIONS

PET DOGS DEMOCRATIC PARTY MANIFESTO

Employment and pensions are at the very heart of all that is wrong with how we are treated. Whether a dog works as a pet, a sniffer dog, or as an assistance dog he or she is fulfilling an important role and it is time for that to be recognised. A pat on the head is not adequate recompense for our labours, and, despite what a Spaniel might tell you, neither are the words 'Good dog.' Being paid for our labours is an important step towards independence and dignity. We are not slaves, dependent on the whim of a master. We are free dogs with rights that need to be upheld.

Wages

The PDDP adopted the slogan 'Minimum wage for working dogs' very early in our campaigning. Extending the laws on the minimum wage and the working time directive to cover all dogs as well as humans, is an essential requirement. The only difference between us and humans is the age these regulations should take full effect. There are seven dog years to every one human year and so the full minimum wage for dogs will apply from 2 years and 6 months old and not 18 years of age, which would clearly be ridiculous as we rarely live that long.

It is also time to see an end to the current system where, if there is any payment, money goes to the dog's human and not the dog himself. At present there is no protection for the dog as to how the money is used. This is often the case in the acting profession. Fellow dogs, wake up, you are being pimped by your humans. We must demand the right to have our wages paid directly into our own bank accounts. In turn those accounts should be accessed only by our own pawprint, retina scan, or microchip. I guess we need to start with legislation which forces banks to allow us to open our own bank accounts first, so there may be several steps in the process.

Working hours
The Working Time Directive would be the same as for humans and no dog should be forced, cajoled, or bribed with a game of fetch, to sign a waiver to the contrary. It is barbaric that assistance dogs are on call 24 hours a day, even when sleeping and receive no assigned rest periods or holidays. How can they possibly work at their optimum capability in conditions like that? It is taking 'will work for food' several pawprints too far. These courageous dogs are lifesavers and need time off as any other dog does.

The introduction of these laws may increase the number of jobs for guide dogs and hearing dogs as they will need to work a shift system, so as not to be in breach of the maximum hours. With this in mind there will be funding of these important services from taxes and they will not have to rely solely on the generosity of public donations for their training.

Further discussion will be needed about the working hours of dogs who are pets in a one pet household. Clearly, where a family is particularly demanding the dog will need to be given time off from providing relaxation therapy and entertaining children. These roles can be very stressful and demanding, particularly where the children are young and boisterous.

Pension
Dog pensions should be provided by the state at the age of nine human years (63 to us). As bigger dogs have a much shorter life expectancy, but by contrast need to eat more,

the pension should be graded by size of dog. Now don't get me wrong, this should not mean that dogs that let themselves go and have a lifetime of overeating will then benefit from a higher pension. The grades should be based on the ideal weight for the breed or general dog size, perhaps with our own equivalent of the Body Mass Index. On this basis a St Bernard would receive decidedly more than a Yorkshire Terrier, but the terrier would receive a lower figure for their long and often spoilt retirement. Some dogs might, sadly, not reach retirement age and in that case there should be an amount paid to any dependent puppies and an amount paid to their human to cover a decent burial in the corner of the garden with a suitably inscribed statue of the beloved dog to go over it.

Having a discussion on whether a pension should be based on final salary or defined contributions is all rather irrelevant if you don't have any income to base either of them on in the first place. It is shocking that dogs are exploited in this way. Fine, so most humans do buy us the things we need and do look after us into our old age, but not all of them do. We are intelligent creatures and should be trusted to make decisions on our own expenditure. There should be a basic non-contributory state pension for dogs, with any additional employment pension on top of that.

I take my collar off to organisations such as Nottinghamshire Constabulary who, without pressure from ourselves, introduced pensions to its retired service dogs to assist with the care they might need. This needs to be made a nationwide policy and not one applying to a minority of dogs.

Unemployment

Dog unemployment is a much harder issue. Once you accept that being a pet is itself a full time job, and should be appropriately rewarded, you are left with all those stray dogs and dogs in shelters who are without a home or employment. All dogs who find themselves in these positions should be able to claim basic benefits to keep themselves alive. They should not face euthanasia simply because they cannot pay their way. They have a right to self-determination and whilst they might choose to continue to sleep on the streets they could at least afford to pay for essential medical care and regular meals without scavenging. For those who throw themselves upon the state for aid, they could perhaps be asked to earn some of their benefit by providing essential services such as hospital therapy, although (and this is the only time you will hear me say this) it would not be unreasonable to ask them to have a bath first.

Being able to support ourselves is about the real quality of life issues. How many humans get to a point where the cost of treating us becomes too high? If we were able to save for our old age and ill health then, in the absence of a free national dog health service, we could fund our own treatment and make our own decisions on whether we wanted to stay with mainstream treatment or try complementary therapies. It is unfair that simply because income is withheld from us, these are decisions we are in no position to make.

If these policies are not brought about through the ballot box then it is perhaps time for dogs to consider their position with regards to going on strike. Could we actually bring the country to its knees? Imagine the role reversal of having your human begging you to go back to your role as pet. Obviously guide dogs and other assistance dogs would be like the emergency services and would still have to work. The same would be true of sniffer dogs looking for explosives. However, sheepdogs, hunting dogs, dogs used in animal testing and cart-dogs could all go on strike without causing any serious issue. Pets could withdraw their therapy services from the family for a period of time, although in some families that may come under the same category as emergency services! The most effective might be the hunting dogs as they are more likely to directly affect the ruling classes.

If we take our protest to this level we may be accused of demanding change with menaces, but only if we bare our teeth. Humans might try to unnerve us by calling these random protests 'wild-cat strikes', but this is a cause worth fighting for. It is our future that is on the line.

See also Discrimination.

FOREIGN POLICY AND DEFENCE

Both foreign policy and defence are very important to dogs, but in a completely different way than they are to humans. We are by nature territorial and wow betide the dog, or cat that strays into what we perceive as 'our patch'. However, when we fight, we resort to no more than paw to paw combat, a lot of barking and the occasional flying attack with teeth bared and ready to bite. We do not resort to guns, tanks or nuclear missiles. In general our approach is to bark at it, claw it, bite it or pee on it and if we can't do any of those we walk, or slink, away. Our equivalent of waving a white flag is to roll over and concede.

There are few things we think worth fighting for. Food and territory are the main ones. We will protect our pack and our young against invasion, but we rarely try to take over another dog's territory. Can you imagine, as a human, sitting down to your evening meal and then seeing a strange dog, nonchalantly walking up and curling up next to the table? It just doesn't happen. If your house and garden are little Fluffy's home you won't suddenly find Cindy the Elkhound has moved in and taken over her place.

We can be amicable as long as we know the rules and can sniff each other. Like humans we play games to hone our fighting skills but we rarely go out looking for trouble. On the whole, our defence strategy is probably best summed up as 'leave us alone and we'll leave you alone too'. If all else fails, I would plan to send in my housemate Shadow. NO ONE crosses Shadow. She rules with a rod of iron and has to do no more than give another dog 'one of her looks' for it to fall into line. I've often wondered how she does it, but I think for that look to work it has to be backed up by the belief that, if they don't comply she will do something far worse. Trust me, I've been on the receiving end and you really don't want to cross her. I can't help but wonder if she ought to offer training to some of the human world leaders. Disputes could be settled so much more easily if the Queen, for example, could turn up in a war zone and just give the aggressor's troops 'one of those looks' so that they would slink away and leave everyone in peace.

Foreign Policy
We enjoy travelling as much as the next animal, although

frankly it does make us nervous and the reassurance of familiar surroundings helps us to stay more relaxed. Whereas humans go to places like the Costa Del Sol and recreate home so they don't feel too nervous, we prefer to simply stay at home most of the time. Having good relations with other countries is important to us though and we are more than happy to work with them. The PDDP's preferred alliances are Belgium (where I was born) and Switzerland (my ancestral homeland), but to be honest, as long as the people smell ok, we'll form alliances with just about anyone.

Country and regional borders will be marked carefully by being peed on with regular markers. Lampposts and trees will be placed specifically for the purpose.

We will withdraw from the EU and form new alliances with those countries that uphold the rights of dogs. There will be free trade with both Belgium and Switzerland (they are my friends) but import duties will be levied on anything brought in from anywhere else. I realise that may mean we have lots of chocolate, but are missing a few other essentials, but that is a sacrifice that will have to be made. In fairness, we can't eat the chocolate, but it should help to keep the humans happy with the arrangement.

Under no circumstances will we trade with countries which eat dog. We will put in place any restrictions within our power to apply pressure for this practice to be stopped. We will also offer asylum to all our canine comrades wishing to flee from those countries. They could perhaps be classified as 'culinary refugees' instead of 'political' ones, unless one regards being eaten as a purely political issue. It really does go to show the importance of universal suffrage for dogs, so that we can elect a party that will immediately ban the eating of our kind. I'm not sure that I would advocate a branch of the PDDP being started in countries which do eat dogs, the members might be too obvious a target. It would be a very brave dog that stood up and announced his candidature for government. He might be considered something of a delicacy.

We will not get involved in matters of sovereignty. Our policy on this is clear, countries should be free to make their own decision as to who they are allied with and no country shall belong to another one, except where it has been bought up as part of a commercial transaction or through being taken over as a result of bankruptcy and therefore being bought out. Ownership of countries shall not be determined by war.

Defence

Dogs in the armed services are the real heroes. The battles they fight are not even their battles, but those of the humans around them and yet they serve tirelessly, often being injured in the combat. On occasion they give their lives in service to their country. Many dogs work tirelessly throughout the year, keeping our countries safe from terrorists so that we pet dogs can live in comfort and security. These dogs should be recognised for their service and provided with every comfort known to canine kind.

Where dogs are caught up in human war zones we should be taking action on their behalf. Obviously, our borders should be open for them to seek refuge. but we should go further than that and send in our own peace keeping forces or even go as far as peeing on their oppressors.

We will not maintain a nuclear deterrent, for a start we don't know how they work, but mainly because it is not our style. We might send in the odd skunk, or my housemate, Shadow, after she has eaten something which has disagreed with her, but that is as far as we are prepared to go towards biological warfare.

We will declare the country to be neutral and demand a 250 mile exclusion zone around all our shores and airspace to be kept free from combat or any form of military activity. Now I realise that that encompasses the whole of Belgium, most of the Netherlands and large parts of France amongst others but we'd like to think they would come round to seeing things from our perspective and respect our right to a peaceful existence.

In the event of a human conflict, no dog should be forced to take sides or serve. Neutrality shall be maintained at all levels whether household or national, unless there is food at stake.

For restrictions on movement see immigration

IMMIGRATION

Immigration should be open to any dog who can demonstrate that he or she has a home to go to and the means to support him or herself for the coming years, even in ill health.

State benefits will not be available to immigrant dogs during the first five years of residency unless they have come as an asylum seeker in the 'culinary' category or as a result of leaving a war zone to which it is not yet safe for them to return.

The indignity and iniquity of the present travel restrictions will be lifted and made consistent with those of humans. This may be addressed by some of the current requirements for animals being extended to humans – see below.

No country shall require tattooing in addition to microchipping. Having your ear tattooed should be available as a fashion statement for those who like pain and should not be a means of identification. We are dogs with names. We are not numbers.

The practice of microchipping, which is being made compulsory, will continue only on condition that the dog's human is also microchipped and is therefore easily identifiable and easy to find. Humans will suffer the indignity of having their chips read on any occasion they wish to return to the UK, so should be careful as to where the chip is inserted! In the unfortunate event of their chip moving around their body, which I can assure you does happen, they may need to be prepared to face an all over body scan. Incidentally, have you seen the size of the needle that injects the microchip? It is not for the faint hearted. Alternatively if a retina scan is good enough for a human it should be good enough for a dog and has the advantage that it does not rely on something which is easily lost or able to malfunction.

With regards to the microchipping legislation, whilst they have covered the need to keep the details of the chip up to date, I can only hope they have thought about the situation in which the chip fails. At those times it would be inappropriate for them to hold either an owner, or their dog, responsible. My housemate Shadow has personal experience of chips failing and whatever the authorities tell you, it does happen.

The PDDP will also ensure that there are no powers of 'stop and search' to check a dog's chip without a good reason to do so. A good reason is not that the dog came running when offered a treat either! If the dog is genuinely lost and has asked for help in finding his or her human, or has committed a crime and been read his rights, including being offered the opportunity of having his or her lawyer present, then it is reasonable for their chip to be checked, but not otherwise. We are not second class citizens who can be treated with less respect just because we walk on four legs.

If rabies vaccinations are to be compulsory for dogs to be able to travel, and I can see the sense in that, there is no reason why humans should not be vaccinated against any disease which may be passed to dogs before they too are allowed to travel. The current requirement to wait three weeks after vaccination shall also be applied to humans. The waiting time should be lifted for small puppies leaving their mother for the first time as long as their mother and any other resident dogs are fully vaccinated. It would be far better if young pups travelling abroad for their first home were able to do so when still young enough to find the changes easy to adapt to, instead of being nearly four months old. Following on from this, those pups would need to be in the ownership of their new human in the UK before travelling. This would prevent the risk of puppy farmers sending young pups to the UK with forged papers. The regulations for travel need to be written with suitable exceptions and not be a one size fits all blanket policy. There can be good reasons for young pups to travel, where for example it belongs to a vulnerable breed which is trying to widen its gene pool in the UK. Legitimate owners should not be penalised by the need for legislation to prevent puppy farming.

With regards to the requirement for a dog to be wormed before travelling, don't even get me started on the indignity of being force fed a worming tablet. You just see if you like it. It is barbaric. Have they not heard of the hygiene hypothesis and how being too clean is proving bad for the health? Ok, so the worms we normally get are the wrong type of worms to be good for us, but that's not the point. Humans are taking away our rights to be dirty and it isn't constructive.

At least now we don't have to have a vet signing to say we are healthy to travel. In reality it would be much more pleasant to travel if every human with coughs and colds were made to stay at home rather than being allowed to sneeze and cough all over you in the course of the journey. I think here rather than abolishing the requirement it should be reintroduced and then I would simply like to see the same regulations applied to humans.

I was thinking that a way to stop puppy farming abroad, where puppies are then smuggled into the UK illegally, would be to deport the puppies back to their countries of origin. Of course it may be difficult to get them to say exactly where they have come in from, and in fairness some of them may not know. However if their originating countries were overrun by puppies it might help to get them to clean up the conditions that some of these young dogs are having to grow up in. We would need to address puppy farming in the UK as well, but that will need a different approach involving long prison sentences for the humans involved where they have to live in the same sorts of conditions that they subjected the dogs to.

Dogs, when travelling, should always be permitted to travel in proximity to their human. That may mean they need a seat on the plane or that they go up on deck on a ship, but they should never be treated as cargo and made to travel in substandard conditions as though they are nothing better than a parcel or a suitcase. We need someone to hold our paw when we are scared as much as anyone does, quite apart from the difficulty of breathing in the hot and airless cargo conditions. Having us in the cabins will have the added advantage of our helping to calm stressed passengers and provide therapy on route. On long haul flights adequate toilet facilities would be required. This could be a simple post and fake grass in standard class and real turf and a small tree in the first class cabin.

HEALTHCARE

The provision of healthcare and how it is paid for is a universal issue. There are many countries in which the provision for all species is inadequate, including humans. I, however, am looking at the provision of care here in the United Kingdom and advocate that as with the humans' National Health Service there should be a National Pet Health Service covering all our needs regardless of our ability to pay. This should extend to dental care as well. Generally as long as we look after them, our teeth do last a lifetime so the dental provision may not need to be excessive. There may need to be proportionately higher numbers of Dental Hygienists to help with advice and cleaning our teeth, rather than dentists. I don't see us being fitted with false teeth if we lose the odd one, and we don't often need fillings. To be fair we would reintroduce a greater provision of NHS dental care for humans too, we're not looking to perpetuate the current species distinction, although we may draw the line at cats and piranha are definitely excluded. Dental care could also include the issue of free chews to help us clean our teeth naturally.

More should be invested into research of conditions relating to dogs and in testing to ensure the products used on us are suitable for us specifically. Just because something works on humans does not mean that it will work in exactly the same way on us. I would particularly urge the investment of money into research to find an

PET DOGS DEMOCRATIC PARTY MANIFESTO

alternative way of delivering the Kennel Cough vaccine.

No dog likes having that squirted up their nose. That really cannot be the only way it can be delivered effectively.

Anal thermometers should be outlawed. Someone needs to develop a good thermometer that can take an accurate reading in a dog's ear, however hairy it is, to spare us the indignity of finding ourselves with a piece of glass stuck an inch up our rear end… and worse if we inadvertently sit down while our temperature is being taken.

All routine vaccinations should be provided to every dog, so that none of us suffers because our human has run out of money and we are bottom of the list. If humans have the opportunity to be vaccinated against common conditions that affect their health then we should have the same basic right. Opting out should be at the sole discretion of the dog and not the human.

Obviously, in order to make the budget stretch there may need to be some prioritisation of treatment. Some people say that conditions caused by our own stupidity or lack of will-power should not be treated at the public expense, but let's face it, how does that differ from some of the ridiculous injuries people turn up with at Accident and Emergency, or, for that matter, many of the arrivals at the maternity unit? Being realistic we have to accept that there is a great deal of stupidity in the world and it may not have been distributed evenly, in fact most of us suffer from it in one form or another.

I would also like to do something about waiting rooms. Very often, so I am told, doctors' waiting rooms have toys for children to play with. Why aren't there toys for us to play with in the vets' waiting room? I grant a heated game of tug may become a little inconvenient and the cats might lose on a regular basis, but I see the latter point as a bonus. Of course, in my experience cats rarely play fair and while you are busy tugging they have a nasty tendency to swipe you with their claws. In my book that's cheating, but I guess that's a cat for you, but I digress. I'm sure there are toys which could be found to suit all of us while waiting nervously to see the vet.

The healthcare issue becomes particularly poignant when we approach the end of our natural lives and our humans are faced with difficult decisions about how much they can afford to pay to put right the problems we face. Life or death decisions should NEVER be a question of money. They should only ever be a question of what is best for the pet. I'll come back to the problem of compulsory euthanasia. I need to compose myself first. It's a very emotive subject for all of us.

I was wondering, are dogs at risk from any type of flu pandemic? Can it be passed to dogs? If it can, we commit to building up sufficient supplies of vaccines and antiviral drugs to cover the whole of the dog population as well as humans. If, of course, we are safe from the possibility of transfer, then we dogs will volunteer for all those jobs that humans will need us to do, such as nursing. We could run the centres that people have to go to into in order to collect their drugs. We could keep the country going in the event of a pandemic. Thinking about it, it would be a perfect time for us to undertake a coup and seize the running of the country. I could declare myself as Prime Minister, without going through an election; although that may be seen as taking advantage of the situation.

I want to talk about something that you will find utterly horrific. In your history studies, you will have come across some very bad people that have at times had policies of compulsory euthanasia for their fellow humans. You will have found this shocking, as indeed it is, but what the books don't mention is that humans have been allowed to undertake compulsory euthanasia on my fellow dogs without any redress whatsoever. There should be no compulsory euthanasia. Many an elderly or sick dog could still live out his days happily with twenty-four hour nursing care. Euthanasia, as with humans, should only ever be voluntary and a choice we make when the pain gets too much for us to bear. The life of an animal should never be ended as a means of convenience to humans. I realise incontinence in an elderly dog is hard to deal with, but I'm sure there must be an equivalent of the pants that humans can use when faced with that embarrassing problem. They could be made in all sizes for all types of house animals and perhaps in colours to match our fur.

It is uncommon for a dog not to be in sound mind at the end of his or her life. We generally retain our faculties longer in relative terms than humans, but in the unlikely event that we cannot make the decision about euthanasia then our human should be able to make the decision for us, in conjunction with a vet we trust and taking into account the degree of pain or unhappiness we have reached. In turn if we are around when our humans are sick, we should be able to make that decision on their behalf!

However, aside from the emotive consideration of a dog reaching the end of his natural life what I am talking about is where, simply because no home can be found for the dog, they are put to sleep so that they don't inconvenience humans. It's barbaric. There are humans who are a great inconvenience but they are allowed to live, so why not us dogs?

BREEDING

This is another very emotive issue amongst dogs and one that we need to give adequate attention to. I know that the human political parties do not cover breeding, at least not in this country, but perhaps they should. Every nation needs a new generation of fit and healthy puppies every few years if it is to survive and prosper. You only have to look at the problems of the aging human population to realise that is true. Someone has to pay for the old age of the last generation, unless the country has the sense to put savings aside to cover the future and even then they'd need to be able to buy in young people to look after them.

With dogs, breeding issues are more difficult. Oh, if we were all just mutts it would be easier, but we have distinct groups rather like ethnic groups, that we want to preserve for the future and that's where it gets complicated. With some of our breeds it is human intervention that has messed things up in the first place, for others... well it's complicated.

It is wholly unfair that we pedigree dogs can only breed if we are considered perfectly fit and look just right, while humans and for that matter mongrels are allowed to get on with it without any intervention whatsoever. If every human that didn't look quite right, or who had a heart murmur or the possibility of developing a genetic disease were precluded from having children then the human race would be a much smaller thing, although better looking and potentially healthier!

I do appreciate that there are humans who might say that if we don't want our pedigrees registered we could just get on with it anyway. However, there are parallels with humans. Can you imagine, in the United Kingdom, if anyone who was likely to appear in Burke's Peerage had to comply with the testing we go through? It would be a sure way of reducing the size of the aristocracy! I wonder exactly what proportion would be ruled out if the upper classes were not allowed to be more than 5% inbred and had to be tested for both health conditions and temperament before being allowed to have children!

It turns out that having puppies is not a right. I know that is a hard truth to bear, but there is no right to procreate successfully. Of course it is instinctive and we'd all like to be able to be a proud parent, but it just doesn't work that way. In nature there can be good reasons why it is unsuccessful and although science has provided ways to overcome many of the problems it won't always work. There are times when having puppies is wrong. No dog really wants to pass on to his or her offspring genetic conditions which are going to cause distress throughout their lives. The Kennel Club applies certain restrictions to what we pedigree dogs are able to do and I argue that either these need to be lifted or they should be applied to all dogs and to humans alike. In fairness I think it should be the latter.

For all dogs and humans, health testing for key genetic health conditions should therefore be encouraged. If parents have full knowledge that they may pass on a debilitating condition to their offspring then they should be tested before breeding and make decisions in full knowledge in choosing their partner in the same way that we have to. None of this marrying for love, it's time to be practical in choosing your mate. You want to make sure they have traits that will be complementary to yours as well as health. If your ears stick out you should mate with a partner with good ears to give the offspring a fighting chance of looking ok. If your back is too long, find someone who has a shorter back to balance it out. At least then the system would be equally punitive to everyone.

Inbreeding should be kept to a minimum – ok to be fair humans haven't been guilty of the same levels of inbreeding, at least not in recent times, but it's caused problems in health for many breeds and needs to be discouraged. You might think your aunt smells nice, but just remember what it might do to the puppies. If not with humans, these principles should definitely apply in the world of cross-breeds and mongrels as well as pure-bred dogs.

For registered pedigree dogs there is a lower and an upper age limit for our having puppies. The same would be a good idea for humans and mongrels. If you scaled it up directly for our breed then the lower age would be 14 human years and the upper age would be 56. That seems quite a broad enough period to me. Our girls are only allowed one pregnancy a year as well and no more than four in total. Now, I'm not suggesting that humans should only have one child ever seven years. I can see that might be impractical but maybe the maximum number of pregnancies might work – although of course that can result in up to 40 or more puppies in some breeds and I don't think that would be a good idea for humans.

Mongrels and cross-breeds face a different set of problems. They are very often neutered against their wishes and this does not seem fair. Instead, in order for them to have puppies mongrels should have the health tests of all that breeds that make them up. That should keep them occupied for a while and cut down on the level of unwanted puppies. Although they should probably be character tested too, I can't help thinking that it is in fact their humans who should be being tested to make sure they have a suitable character. In my experience a dog's temperament is as likely to be affected by how he or she is brought up by the humans in their life as it is by their parents.

Now I know I may be contradicting myself here and

have said above that choosing your partner for love is not appropriate, but dogs do need to have more say in who their partner will be and be able to choose for themselves where possible. My housemate, Shadow, has had no say in who will be the fathers of her puppies or for that matter when she will have them. To be fair, when they are in season, bitches will mate with just about anything on four legs that comes their way, but it is time for us to take some control back from humans in the decision making process. I would suggest that the bitch be allowed to set up her own 'speed dating' type process BEFORE she comes into season to select a mate. She should have enough time with each male to ask important questions such as 'how does he expect to provide for their family?' and 'will he be around to help with the night-time feeds?' The bitches should also be looking carefully at the long term career prospects of the dogs, including opportunities for promotion and of course not forgetting their actual level of take home pay and the availability of a pension.

The practice of making pedigree dogs mate with different dogs each time, and preventing them from forming lasting and meaningful monogamous relationships is unjust and should be outlawed. Ok, so we may choose to mate with anything and everything, but we should have the right to choose. There may be dogs out there who long for commitment, but we don't have the opportunity to form a proper relationship as the next time we mate we have to meet a different dog. I accept there are humans that live like that, but they do it by choice – we don't! I've got brothers and sisters that I don't even know about.

Then there are the problems of dogs in straightened circumstances. Dogs are not simply discouraged from having puppies if they can't afford to bring them up. We are physically assaulted so that we can't. Can you imagine the uproar if every unemployed human were neutered to make sure they didn't add to their problems? It is a contravention of our basic canine rights. No dog should be neutered without his or her written agreement. There are some vets who push owners to have their dogs neutered even when they intend to allow them to breed. This sort of pressure is unwarranted and should not be allowed. Our feelings should be taken into account and more credit given to us in our ability to make sensible decisions. Where neutering does go ahead, we should have access to counselling to help us come to terms with the prospect that we will never have puppies of our own. That's true really for both dogs and humans who find they cannot have children. Counselling might well be helpful to them to deal with the issue, although humans often deal with it by getting a dog, but what are we supposed to do?

Prostitution
I have left to last the question of prostitution. It is no small concern. Humans are pimping male dogs and pocketing the proceeds. I am being serious here, it is a major worry. They are actually charging girl dogs a fee to have sex with their male dogs and in some cases it is quite a lot of money. I've already explained that, when they are in season, girls are victims of their urges and will mate with anything. That is not the time for them to be making rational decisions. Of course they are going to hand over their life savings if a human offers them a good looking male. It is an abuse of the tender state they find themselves in and even more of an abuse of the male dogs.

I am not saying that the male dogs should be prevented from charging for their services. It always sounded quite a good life until the opportunity was removed from me and I had to turn to politics instead. It is not as though the stud dogs even get to see a share of the proceeds. Oh, they have a good time along the way, but what about the money and saving for a better future? They can't be stud dogs forever. Hard as it is to accept, looks and fertility decline with time. They need to be able to build up a retirement fund and have a second string career to fall back on.

Puppies
As with breeding, I realise this is not a section you see in most human political manifestos. Obviously it would be headed 'children' rather than 'puppies' if it were. However, there are practices which are applied to dogs which are scandalous and it is our duty to fight against these.

The Ethics of Selling Children
The ethics of selling human children is one which has been addressed in this country. Where children are raised in surrogate conditions or for adoption there is a restriction on how the finances of those situations are handled. All parties must be in agreement for one thing. Payments are designed to cover expenses and not to be a mainstream commercial transaction. Tempting as it may be for many parents, it is not permitted, for example, to put your children up for sale on Ebay or Amazon. The days in which humans can be sold legally has long since passed in civilized countries. I know there is still human trafficking, but it is illegal and great lengths are taken to

prevent it. So why is it legal to sell our children?

Puppies can be sold for any amount without restriction and without the consent of either of the parents. In some cases the parent leaves the room to go to the bathroom and comes back to find, in their absence, one of their children has been sold to a new home. It is nothing short of slavery. We are not a commodity which can be bought and sold at will. We are sentient beings who care about our families. Oh there are times when, in common with humans, we'd gladly sell our puppies. They come home with tattoos, or having had a fight with the local tom cat, gashes across their noses and chunks of ear missing, and never mind sell them, we'd give them away, but those moments pass and, like humans, we remember how much we love them.

Obviously, once we gain independence, and are earning a wage for the services we provide, it will be a lot easier for us to argue we can effectively support our families and keep them together, but under the present system it is not as though we receive the money. Oh I know that any good breeder who does all our health tests will tell you that they don't really make any money out of it and are probably in a loss situation, but we should be in a position to manage our own funds and decide for ourselves whether our children stay with us. At the very least if they do go to learn the trade of being a pet we should be able to ensure that their terms and conditions are acceptable and they will be taking home a living wage.

We should be able to make sure that at least one of the puppies stays at home to look after us into our old age.

Absentee Fathers
It is a tragic state of affairs that very few puppies grow up

with a father in their lives. In most cases, me included, we never even meet our fathers. I was at least in regular contact with mine before he died and I knew he cared about me, but that is not true for most puppies. 'Every puppy needs a Dad' – it is one of our key slogans. Who else is there to show a young dog how to cock his leg? Our poor single mothers do their best to bring us up, but male puppies, in particular, need a role model to take heed of. Without question, growing up around both parents does, in most cases, make things less stressful for the mother. There are two parents to keep the litter in line and show them the right ways to behave. Is it any wonder that so many dogs end up with behavioural problems when so few grow up in a two parent household? Now don't get me wrong, I'm not saying it's right for the parents to stay together for the sake of the puppies and it is never good for a mother to stay in an abusive relationship, but not many dogs even try to stay together much past the day of mating, let along until the puppies are born. That wasn't how it was in the wild. When we lived in packs our fathers were around. We looked after the older generations and shared in the care of the young. Now in this so called 'civilized' society our poor mothers are expected to cope alone.

This is not just an issue relating to the mongrels of the dog world. Shockingly, pedigree fathers are no more commonly found taking their responsibilities seriously than any cross-breed or stray. It is not just that the father does not live in the same household, he rarely even visits his children, let alone takes them for trips to McDonald's on Saturdays. Nor do most absent fathers pay maintenance for the upkeep of their children. As I said before, they, or at least their humans, may have been on the receiving end of funds from the mother, but still walk away long before the children are born.

I'm sure this is one of the reasons so many mothers have to send their puppies off to new homes when they are barely more than eight weeks old. They simply can't afford to take care of the puppies themselves. Oh don't get me wrong, some of those homes are very good and it is not as though the puppies are not well looked after, but they earn their keep by offering pet services and have to cope, sometimes never seeing their mother again. Some mothers do manage to arrange visits to their children and that is great when it can happen, but the whole system needs to be looked at so that the mother isn't forced to give her children away in the first place.

All puppies should have access rights to both parents and absentee fathers should pay maintenance, direct to the mother for the care of their puppies, until those puppies reach adulthood. I suppose we will need to set up a Puppy Support Agency to track down absent fathers, or in some case mothers, and then try to get them to make payments.

CRIME AND PUNISHMENT

Crime and punishment is an emotive subject in any culture. It is time that we were judged against appropriate standards for our species and not against those set by humans. Eating food from a plate that has been left within reach, and which we have not been specifically told is not for us, is not theft. It is simply making the most of an opportunity. Digging in the garden is not a crime. Humans dig with a spade, we dig with our paws, it is as much our garden as it is theirs if they have invited us to live there and we are providing pet services to them. I am not going to go through every perceived crime, although I will mention a few specifically, however humans need to remember that we are dogs and if they have asked a dog to live with them then they must be prepared for him or her to behave as a dog. If they want us to be more alike, then I suggest they adopt more dog-like behaviours and stop expecting us to become human. I have a slogan 'Dog enough not to be human, human enough to be a pet' perhaps humans should meet us half way.

Peeing in the house
Some offences should be taken off the statute book, or at least be worded differently. Peeing on the carpet as a puppy, when the human has forgotten to take the puppy out at regular intervals and has not taken the time to show him where to pee, is not a crime. It is not something we should be punished for. It is the human's fault. Humans put their babies in nappies until they can control their bladder for longer intervals, the least they can do is understand it takes us a while to build up to being able to wait several hours between pees.

Peeing on the carpet as an elderly dog is not a crime. As humans get older they need to go to the bathroom more often and so do we. These are not things we should be punished or shamed for. Provide us with an inside toilet or make it easy for us to go outside when we need to.

Peeing on the clean washing very deliberately, because I'd been told off, probably was a crime and I can see that should be treated differently.

Leaving Dog Hair Around
Shedding our hair, so humans end up wearing it, is not a crime. When did our human last brush us? Do humans have any idea how much of their hair and dead skin there

is down here on the floor, where, most of the time, they make us lie down (see below re sleeping on the couch)? If humans don't want to wear dog hair then they should get a Poodle – although frankly if I were them I'd put up with the hair! A Poodle may not leave hair around, but they will hog the mirrors when getting ready to go out and will invariably be the last one ready to leave the house.

Sleeping on the Couch

Getting onto the couch and making ourselves comfortable is not a crime. Oh yes, we're used to lying on the floor, but which of the humans amongst you faced with the choice of comfort or deprivation would choose the hard option? And I'm specifically excluding monks, and men who think that camping is a 'bonding experience', in that last question. We are asking for equality here. Yes, there are times humans choose to sit on the floor and there will be times the floor is also our choice, but we demand the right to sit on the couch without fear of punishment. Especially as we get older and our joints aren't what they were, then we need somewhere a little softer to rest our aging limbs.

Chasing the Cat

Why would humans get a cat if it were not as a toy for us to chase? Being clawed round the nose when we manage to get too close is bad enough, we don't need humans chipping in with extra punishment. Oh we might knock a few things off as we chase round, but that's the cat's fault. Have you seen the way they squeeze through gaps that aren't there and jump over tables to get away? We can't possibly be blamed if the route we have to take to catch them involves knocking the human's best china vase off the sideboard. They should tell the cat to play fair.

Of course, my threatening behaviour towards the baby rabbit might well be viewed as a crime and in retrospect it was quite wrong of me to think of it in terms of how much chewing it would involve. Thankfully the rabbit was returned to the shop for its own safety and my crime was only one of plotting a murder rather than carrying it out. I do know of dogs who coexist quite happily with small animals and I do promise that if any join the party I will leave dealing with them to my colleagues and will refrain from being involved.

The Dangerous Dogs Act

There is one very serious and important subject that I need to cover in this section and that is the Dangerous Dogs Act. This is a very badly planned and ill thought through piece of dogist legislation. It has been brought about to prevent specific problems, but in so doing, no thought has been given to the wider implications of the act or the potential effect on dogs in general. This act should be abolished and replaced with legislation that reflects the same principles as other human legislation and I am really being serious now.

Under the existing legislation a dog can be accused of being seriously out of control by a human who only fears that to be the case. No consideration is taken to the phobias and sensitivities of the human, so it is possible for an over sensitive human, and we all know some of those, to report a dog who to anyone else would be considered perfectly innocent. If it were just a question of reporting then there would not be a major problem, but it is what happens next which is where the injustice begins.

Being wrongly accused is difficult for anyone. However, a human accused of a crime is, under English law, innocent until proven guilty. A dog accused under the Dangerous Dogs Act is guilty unless the complaint can be disproved. It is outrageous. The onus of proof is completely the wrong way round.

It gets worse. If accused, we are taken into custody. Separated from our humans and they are not even allowed to know where we are or visit us. There is no bail. No Habeas Corpus as applies to humans and no right to legal representation.

Even on circumstantial evidence it is possible for a dog to face the death penalty. If, for example, a dog is accused of biting someone, there is no requirement for a full medical examination of the human to confirm that a) there is a wound and b) the wound was caused by the dog that has been accused. If it cannot be proved that the dog was not in the vicinity at the time, if witnesses cannot be found who specifically saw what happened and can vouch for the fact that it was not the accused dog then the dog is deemed to be guilty. This is an abomination. What about checking dental records to see if the wound matches the bite of that particular dog? What about taking testimony from the dog and giving him the opportunity to provide an alibi?

There is no protection for innocent dogs under the Dangerous Dogs Act. With this atrocious piece of legislation any of us could find ourselves wrongfully accused and unable to do much about it. Since it has been extended to cover actions on private property, how long will it be before someone visiting a cute puppy gets a nip and makes a complaint?

In this country if a human is dangerous and even goes as far as killing someone, he is locked up, imprisoned, has his rights taken away. Now with a dog, I'm not defending appalling behaviours when they occur, but in the same situation the dog would have his own life taken away. The death penalty is still in place for us. The reason this is so grossly unfair is that on most occasions the real fault lies with the human for not spending enough time training the young animal. Or for giving the dog a rag doll to play with one minute and leaving it alone with a baby the next minute.

Humans have protection under the law and so should we have protection on an equal footing.

CIVIL LIBERTIES & BASIC CANINE RIGHTS

We need our very own Bill of Rights. At the moment we are second class citizens. I hear people in our country criticising the human rights records of other countries while overlooking these dreadful practices when it comes to dogs. Now I don't want to minimise the importance of standing up against countries whose human rights records are bad, but these are double standards and it's time for them to change! We should stand up against the infringements of rights of man and dog alike.

It may have come to your attention that as dogs we

face a large amount of prejudice. We face inequality, injustice and racial abuse. At the moment we have no redress under the laws in almost any country. Now is the time for us to have equal rights with our best friends. It is time for the Human Rights Act to become the Human and Canine Rights Act and for the Universal Declaration of Human Rights to be extended to cover all species. Of course there are dogs who are far too stupid to take advantage of rights afforded to them, but that doesn't mean that the right should be withheld, any more than it should from a poodle because it wastes all its time checking that its hair is in the right place, or from a human who is ripe for nomination as the village idiot. Rights should be applied to all without prejudice. Now is the time for equality for all dogs, even the little rat like ones that on occasion I may have mistaken for vermin.

Racial abuse
It is hard to know how a dog should be classified, but seeing us as a race will help to highlight the wrongs which are being done. I know we are a species, but in many ways we identify with those classified as racial groupings and therefore claim the same privileges.

At a species level, in this age of political correctness we have woken up to the wrongs being done by using terminology which ridicules or is used to subjugate a particular group, and rightly so. However, terms like 'dog face' as an insult and 'being in the dog house' when somebody is in trouble, are bandied about without thought to the sensitivities and implications for our kind. Now I acknowledge there are positive terms that are associated with us, although they generally refer to our more base instincts and fail to recognise our superior intelligence, but it is time to show respect to canine's everywhere and enshrine this racial equality in law.

The PDDP is also increasingly concerned about the activities of the far right. We recognise all dogs regardless of race or creed to have the same rights and why should people be any different. I have been subject to the odd racist attack by other dogs that don't recognise my breed and I can tell you from personal experience that it is unpleasant and completely unjustified. Why should I be singled out because of the colour of my coat? On the inside, I think just the same and have the same feelings. As far as the claim that dogs from overseas are taking the role of pet that could be going to the English breeds, this is no different from the many English breeds that have happily settled with families abroad. Such freedom of movement should be seen as an opportunity to share each other's cultures and understand each other more fully, not to react aggressively to petty rivalries and insecurities. One of the ironies of the far right talking about people 'going home' is that this is their home and often has been for many generations.

Heritage can be confused. Just because I was born in Belgium does not mean I associate more strongly with Belgium than with anywhere else. I have lived in England for most of my life and both of my parents were actually born in Switzerland. My humans are English and this is where I've made my home.

Segregation

Segregation, discrimination, subjugation and racial abuse have gone paw in hand for centuries. The serious wrong that this gives rise to has been recognised in most of the civilised human world and yet those same humans perpetuate these abuses when it comes to our kind.

We cannot go freely into many public buildings and we are even segregated when it comes to beaches and parks. This canine apartheid is unacceptable in days when around the world so much progress has been made in the name of equality. You need to be aware that this isn't the case in every country. There are countries which welcome us. Countries which truly embrace the idea that man's best friend should be able to go anywhere with him. Of course there are also countries which eat us, but that is a problem that I think we will find even harder to tackle.

What is it exactly that people object to? If it is that my paws are dirty and I could have trodden in anything, then I could put on some slippers or they should be consistent by making humans take their shoes off. If they are concerned that I might go to the toilet on their floor, are they going to also ban toddlers just out of nappies, and babies whose nappies are filled to overflowing? Both of those categories are a much higher risk than I am. Do they think that I may carry some dreadful disease? I probably have more up to date vaccinations than most humans and there are not many diseases that can be transmitted from dog to human. Are they worried about what I will have stuck my nose in? If this is the case, they should also ban small boys who will have had their hands in much the same things. Maybe they are concerned about me deciding to bark, in which case I am definitely not as noisy as most children and many outgoing adults. If they are scared I might attack them then really the question is, 'whatever makes them think they would be that interesting to me?' Besides which, if I am on a lead, exactly how far do they think I am going to get? All in all, the whole thing seems particularly 'dogist' and just goes to show how prejudiced people can be about anyone that is different from themselves.

The Pet Dogs Democratic Party calls for an end to all segregation. It will no longer be legal to ban dogs from parks, beaches, post offices, shops, libraries and hospitals, to name but a few. We understand the desire for cleanliness and advocate that in addition to human toilets, toilets be specifically provided for dogs as well, in addition to dog waste bins with a ready supply of bags for cleaning up after us. We are very happy for the fines for not clearing up to be increased and more rigidly enforced, but we will have the right to go to the same places as our human companions.

This is a country where dogs are referred to as 'man's best friend' and are considered an important part of the family and yet almost everywhere we go we are treated as second class citizens. It is made worse that as a result of human crime it is not even safe for us to wait patiently outside a building for our humans to exit. If we do this we are at risk of all sorts of atrocities and yet it is we who are penalised.

My humans went to a restaurant where they brought the meat round to the table and they could eat as much as they liked. Now is that doggy heaven or what? I would have been prepared to skip the salad bar and just stay sitting at my table quietly waiting for the next lot of meat to arrive. I wouldn't have been any trouble. However, despite my pleadings once again it was explained to me that dogs are not welcome and despite this being the 21st century discrimination and segregation are still rife.

My humans were going to the pictures to see a film. I asked to be included in the trip. I even promised not to keep asking for popcorn, but in another instance of dogist behaviour it turns out that I'm not allowed in the cinema. How is Lassie ever going to develop her fan base if her largest set of followers aren't even allowed into the cinema?

As part of these requirements bars and restaurants will provide clean water bowls for our use. Many parts of Europe are already ahead of us on this and we need to make the UK the dog friendly haven it should be. When we lived in Belgium and were looking for a new car I went to the showroom too. It was important that as the dog of the house I could get in and out easily and was happy with the final decision. Back here in the UK a dog's ideas and considerations are completely overlooked and we are not welcome in the car showroom.

This dogist segregation will be stopped. Showing prejudice against dogs needs to be made a criminal offence as soon as possible.

Universal Suffrage

We have got past the outmoded ideas that women should not be allowed to vote and the inequality that restricted voting to landowners. We have acknowledged that humans as young as 18 should be given the right to vote, no matter how little interest they show. In fact in the recent devolution question even those aged 16 could vote. Now is the time for the right to vote to be extended to all canines over the age of two and half years, which is roughly 18 in human terms.

I recognise that 'One Dog One Vote' might appear wasted on the Toy Breeds, but there is a principal at stake. If a human can vote no matter how weak minded and easily swayed they may be, then the same should be true of dogs too. I also believe that a dog who is incarcerated in

kennels, whether through homelessness or crime should still retain his or her right to vote. For most of them, the Government that is elected will be relevant when they leave their kennel cells and will have a say over their lives. I'd agree a dog suffering from insanity is probably not best placed to elect a sensible Government, but a criminal should not lose his voice. He might be a criminal but he is still a dog and that is what is important. Fair enough remove his right to treats, withdraw his settee and ball thrower, but I do believe that he should retain his right to vote.

Proportional Representation
You would think under a First Past the Post system of election that a dog would beat a human every time, but I'm told it is not about actually racing and that is probably one very good reason why the system should be changed. It also explains why so many MPs are rather elderly. I couldn't see how it was that they had won in racing against a younger candidate.

In reality, as with many new political parties it will be a while before enough people come round to our way of thinking for us to attract a high percentage of the vote. That does not mean we should not be represented. A party that can win 10% of the votes should have 10% of the seats in the Parliament. It seems obvious to me as a dog, so why humans are so slow to comprehend the implications is beyond me. Why would anyone allow themselves to be governed by a party that only gets a third of the votes that are actually cast, but still wins a large majority of the seats? It just does not make sense. Oh I hear you argue that what you want is strong government, but isn't it more important that it is fair and that everyone's voice is heard? What is the point of fighting for universal suffrage if you then accept a system in which the votes of the large majority of people count for nothing?

An election should not be like the 100 metres race

where you are simply trying to find out who is fastest on the day. This is about putting together five years of government for our country. That government should be representative of the wishes of the people and dogs. It is all very well complaining about our current government and saying we need a system that gives us strong leadership instead of coalition, but humans and dogs alike should realise that the current coalition is bringing some balance and stability, even though it is heavily skewed towards the needs of humans. If we were simply following the more uncontrolled policies of the Conservative Party, the cuts would be deeper, the taxes higher and complaints louder. Having a coalition is making sure that the needs of all sectors of society are being heard, except of course dogs as we still aren't represented.

There are educated dogs in every constituency who see our party as the way forward; however our votes count for nothing because we are standing against humans who are all too ready to protect their own self-interest. In actual fact, I don't think we're allowed to stand at all. This isn't the United States where a donkey can be elected Mayor, although some of you in cities of the UK which have mayors may beg to differ on that point. In the UK every law is animalist to keep us in a subjugated position.

I wasn't even sent a polling card when there was the referendum on the Alternative Vote System. I was disenfranchised at a time that really mattered.

Have you stopped to think how much calmer debate might be in the House of Commons with dogs present? I'm sure while he was in Parliament David Blunkett's dog did his best, but he was essentially working to guide Mr Blunkett and would not have been able to spare time for additional therapy for other Members of Parliament. I hope he used his intelligence to ensure his guiding was in the best interests of canines everywhere. He was in the unique position to lead Mr Blunkett through the Aye or Nay channel at voting time as he saw fit, but he wasn't there in his own right so he would have had to be careful he wasn't rumbled.

Obviously the dogs that are elected would need to be well trained and not settle their differences by fighting, but you can see how we could get round the other parties. We would nuzzle up to them when they were stressed and let them stroke us, to calm down. You just see if we can't get our own way after that. It brings a whole new meaning to the idea of schmoozing. It is an approach that is definitely lacking at present. In many ways, I think the women MP's are still missing a trick by not playing on their femininity to get the men to agree to anything they want. You can see it now, a few hundred helpless men, putty in their hands.

There are humans out there who are distorting the truth by trying to say the introduction of the alternative vote system would give us more than one vote. I only wish they were right. What it gives us is our first vote being recognised and counted as meaningful. It gives a voice to those of us who have been ignored for too long. We may not achieve enough MPs to form the next government completely from the Pet Dogs Democratic Party, but what we would have would be the opportunity to voice our policies and hopefully have some of them adopted in exchange for our support in other areas. There is nothing wrong with a coalition government where parties have to listen to each other's views rather than having one party steamrollering proceedings, because with less than half the votes cast they have won more than half the seats in the House of Commons.

It will be one of the top priorities of the Pet Dogs Democratic Party to bring in an appropriate system of proportional representation. I realise that may mean a party led by a Chihuahua could ultimately be represented in Parliament, but that is a risk we have to take.

The Right Not to Have a Bath

We guarantee to all dogs that one of the first things we will see introduced as legislation is the right not to have a bath. No human will make their canine companion bathe to get rid of carefully selected odours that that canine has worked hard to develop. Rolling in fox poo is not a crime and we should not be punished with water torture. If we choose to bathe, and there are some dogs who like swimming and will get in voluntarily, that should be at our discretion and should be in any water of our choosing, no matter its smell or mud like consistency. We are free dogs and capable of making crucial decisions on hygiene for ourselves.

Insisting that I take a bath is a violation of my civil liberties. I reached this realisation when I was last called upon to clean myself up. I protested that I did not like water. I explained that I suffer from eczema, but my protestations were in vain. I had been reassured that I would be thoroughly towelled dry and if I really wanted to I could then have the hair dryer to be absolutely certain I was dry. To be quite honest, I didn't want to. The hair dryer is a very noisy animal and I don't like it. I was given until the afternoon to show I could deal with the problem myself and if that failed then my human would take it upon herself to put me in the shower. I tried to argue that the smell was coming from one of the girls, but as I followed my human around the house, to put my case, the smell followed with us and rather pulled the rug from under my paws. The result was the indignity of a shower and a breach of my Canine Rights. I felt violated.

Indoor Toilets
Modern houses in the Western World have inside toilets. Houses with outside toilets are thought to be in some way sub-standard. So why is it that even when it is raining we dogs are expected to go outside when we need to go to the toilet? Dogs need improved housing. If this were the case for humans they would be described as near slum conditions! It is imperative that toilets are provided indoors for us to use in bad weather, but they should also be provided in good weather too, in the interest of fairness and equality.

These toilets should be clearly marked so as to avoid confusion. How are we to know that a tree brought into the house at Christmas is not our human's present to us to address this dreadful issue? Ok, so the point it gets decorated in tinsel and lights seems to be taking it a bit far, but our expectations have been set, and faced with that thought is there any wonder that we are desperate to christen the tree?

No dog should be forced to live in the poverty and squalor of having to go outside in all weathers to use the toilet.

Freedom of Speech
In 2008 the PDDP adopted as its slogan for the year "Every dog must have his say" and it is important that our right to free speech is enshrined in law. Oh we may

whine a little bit now and again, and are sometimes barking up the wrong tree in the things we come out with, but if it's good enough for humans then it's good enough for us. We need the same rights as our humans with protection of those rights under the law.

Employment Discrimination

Dogs should be given equality in all areas under the law. It should be illegal for any form of discrimination to be shown against us. Incidence of discrimination is insidious. Everywhere you turn there are dogist approaches to life. We will commission a task force to stamp out all areas of discrimination as well as giving dogs full redress under the law.

I was watching the film 'Finding Neverland'. It is a great film, but what I don't understand is why they have a part in a play for a dog which is then played by a human dressed up as a dog. Why not give the part to a real dog? There really aren't enough jobs for dogs without ones that should be for dogs being taken by a human.

Employment legislation is one of the biggest areas of discrimination faced by all species. Now whilst I realise the thought of a 'sniffer cat', or a 'guide ferret for the blind' may not come naturally, it is as important that these roles are opened up as it is that dogs have the opportunity to apply for key roles in the human world. As part of this, animals other than reindeer should have the opportunity to pull Santa's sleigh as long as they have the right skills. I am particularly sensitive about that one as my breed normally pulls a small cart as well as cattle herding and we should be considered for a role with Santa as well as the next cart pulling animal. We might find the flying bit a little difficult, but I don't know too many reindeer that are natural flyers, so I a presuming it is a skill which can be taught.

When advertising for jobs, not only should it not be possible to state the applicant should be a particular sex or racial origin, but it should not be possible to restrict the role to humans. All species who are capable to undertake the role should be entitled to apply and should, if they are the best animal for the job, be recruited on the same basic terms as a human would be. This will take 'equal pay for work of equal value' a whole step change further.

The Right to be a Pet

Although this might slightly contradict my suggestion that 'pet services' should be paid for, I do believe that every dog, working or otherwise, should have the right to a home with a family. If they are not paid to be a pet, then they should be at liberty to decline to allow themselves to be used for stress relief by humans, and should be free to be grumpy if disturbed. What it would mean is that dogs who work in teams for hunting or medical testing should still be able to go home to a cosy fireside for the evening and get all the fuss and attention that comes with being a pet. Of course the antisocial ones can stay in kennels if they prefer, but it should at least be a right and a choice they make for themselves.

The Right to Own Property in Our Own Name

I have heard humans encouraged to make provision for their pets in the event of the human's death and this is very sensible. However, as things stand they are unable to make the only sensible choice of leaving everything directly to Spot or Rover or little Trixie, for them to use or dispose of as they see fit. It is more than a hundred years since the first Married Women's Property Act extended such rights to married women and yet in that time we have made no progress on behalf of either men's or women's canine companions. It's quite an important point when you think how many humans want to leave everything to us in their wills. The Pet Dogs Democratic Party will introduce legislation to enable any dog, over the age of three years, to hold property in his or her own name. Of course, that will necessitate the dog making a will as well. The laws of intestacy could be quite complicated when some male dogs don't actually know what offspring they have and when you try to work out where our human ranks in the order of things. Heaven forbid that on intestacy any of our estate should go to the cat. That if nothing else would drive most dogs to give priority to making a valid will!

Freedom from People Being Mean to Us

Cruelty comes in many forms. Obviously there is outright physical cruelty, which I will come back to, but there is also a wide range of ways in which emotional distress can be inflicted. I know this is a problem for humans as well as dogs, but I can only talk about the canine side.

I watched the film 'The Firm' and it has caused me great emotional distress. Firstly the character and his wife in the film have a lovely pet dog and even when the man hadn't seen it for a few days he didn't make a fuss of it. Poor dog, what kind of human ignores their pet dog when they come home from being away? That was only the beginning of my concerns. At the end of the film when the couple drive off into the sunset, they go without the dog. Where is the dog supposed to be at that point? The humans have left the house for good, they can't just leave their pet behind. Finally there was a very long list of credits of everyone from the cameraman to the casting agent, to the stars to the extras but, although I may be mistaken, I saw no mention of the dog. This is not acceptable.

The more severe forms of cruelty are covered by legislation and that is one of the few areas where the law does look after our interests. However, it needs to go further. One of the heroes of the PDDP is the wonderful man Alan Titchmarsh, who took it upon himself to speak up on our behalf. How good it was to see someone questioning the methods used by Cesar Millan in correcting dogs. I know we can be badly behaved, but there is no need to use things that are little short of torture. Just do the things our mum's do to put is in line. It works remarkably well and doesn't end up causing any pain. It's all very well saying we are pack animals and we need to know our place in the pack, but using an electric shock collar isn't going to earn our respect. It's bullying and we'll do as we are told through fear not through respect – there is a very big difference! I've said before there are things that Cesar Millan says which are very good, but there are many things about us dogs that he has not fully understood. I guess I'm the prime example. When I misbehave it isn't because I need to march across the countryside two steps behind my human, it's because she hasn't had the time to cuddle me and make me feel valued. Now I'm sorry if you think a dog doesn't think that way, but you only have to watch how much better I behave when I've had my morning cuddle than when I don't and you'll realise that having my human's undivided attention and love is what gives me security. Anyway, thank you Mr Titchmarsh, I'm making you an honorary member of the PDDP with immediate effect.

Privacy

Just because we like to greet each other, and often you as well, by having a good sniff around the bottom, it does not mean that we are any less concerned about issues of privacy. For us they manifest themselves in different ways. It is appalling how many humans get away with posting 'shaming' photos of their pets just to make other humans laugh. It is a gross infringement of the rights of the pet. They also sometimes post photos of us in compromising positions, such as in the bath, or asleep. These are invasions of our privacy and we should have recourse to the law. When have any of the dogs among us been asked for our permission for any of these images of us to be used? Our right to privacy should be protected. This may be a society in which issues of privacy are breaking down faster than at any other time, but it does not mean we should not set out to protect the rights of the most vulnerable members of society. A human using social media can select the privacy settings they apply to any images they upload. Where these images are of their pet, then it is the pet who should have control of the image not the human.

I recognise that suing our humans may not be a popular move, but if more respect is not shown to my fellow canines, then it really could come to that.

ARTS AND CULTURE

Arts

It is wholly wrong of humans to assume that as dogs we are not well versed in the Arts. The PDDP is committed to supporting these important areas although in some instances they may take a slightly different form than at present. To be fair, rather than a sculpture made of house bricks you are more likely to find us artistically peeing at different heights and on different sides of a lamppost. We paint with mud rather than paint, usually on the kitchen floor! We tend to howl rather than sing, but it can be just as tuneful. We can even make music if we can lay our paws on enough toys with squeakers at different pitches.

We enjoy all the Arts and are never happier than when having a story read to us while we curl up and relax in front of a log fire.

Just because the art and music we produce is not to your liking, does not make it any less worthy. I fail to understand the desire to listen to indecipherable words in a foreign language at a pitch that rivals nails being dragged down a blackboard, but I don't question your right to listen to it if that is what you choose, although preferably not in my hearing!

In addition to the many worthy areas which currently receive funding, sponsorship will also be given to increase the opportunities for howling concerts as well as the Barking Choir.

On television, Strictly Come Dancing will be replaced

by Strictly Dancing with Dogs as a way to show the potential for humans and canines to work together. One Man and His Dog will be given a primetime slot on one of the major channels and the film channels will be encouraged to show regular viewings of film classics such as Beethoven, Lassie and 101 Dalmatians.

Sports

As with the Arts, sports are important to us, but generally they differ from those undertaken by humans. Under the PDDP fetch will replace football as the national sport and team sports such as flyball will be given funding and moved to some of the current major stadiums, along with agility. However, we are fundamentally opposed to the idea of obedience as a sport and will not be providing any support or funding for this.

Some sports will see a fundamental change to the way they are staged. Dog cart racing will no longer see the human sitting idle while we do all the work. We propose a reversal of roles in which six humans learn to run in unison at high speed pulling the cart being driven by their dog. It might catch on. Once we've mastered this, there will be nothing to stop us moving on to the bob-sleigh and other winter sports. There may need to be some redesign of equipment such as helmets, but that should not be too difficult to achieve.

Traditional dog racing will be disbanded and the greyhounds given the opportunity to be integrated into pet homes. Any dog, regardless of breed will be able to take part in running events, in the same way it works at present for humans. They will not chase a rabbit, in the interests of any family homes which have both dog and rabbit pet members of the household. Any dog who strays off the track out of his lane, or who finds other distractions along the way will be disqualified in the normal way.

The Olympics will feature sports for both dogs and

humans, with some such as discus throwing and fetch being combined in a collaborative effort, although it may be inadvisable for the javelin to be mistaken for the stick retrieving competition and the shot putt should be kept completely separate.

ENVIRONMENT

Forestry
You will not find a party that supports the environment more than we do. We believe that there should be a lot more trees. Trees should be planted everywhere, particularly along places we like to walk. We are committed to reforesting large areas of the British Isles with a variety of species of tree, including a plentiful supply of fruit trees. We probably prefer to plant oak, ash, cedar and beech rather than horse chestnut as those prickly shells can be very uncomfortable under paw and we don't really appreciate the benefits of playing conkers in the same way as humans. There should be more widespread growing of apple and pear trees, particularly those with low hanging fruit that we can reach. Although pine trees smell nice, their needles can be a bit prickly under paw. The only tree we are unlikely to include in the planting is holly. Those leaves are evil!

Wind turbines
There will be no onshore wind farms built on our watch. Have you any idea what those things do to wildlife, never mind to the health of the humans and animals who live within range of them. Even offshore they are a serious threat to sea-birds and should be discouraged. It is not as though they are the answer to all our energy needs. In high winds they have to be turned off and if there's no wind they're no use to anyone, so you can't win.

Solar Power

This will be our preferred method of the provision of power, along with hydro-electric power. However, our requirements for solar panelling will be rather more stringent than has been the case. Solar panels, where fitted to a house, must be the same size as the side of the roof they are fitted to in order to remain aesthetically pleasing. Yes, dogs do care about aesthetics – although frankly we find it quite hard to spell. Ideally, larger buildings like barns with south facing roofs will be fitted with solar panelling, both to power the farm and supply energy to the National Grid. In addition, all flat roofed buildings will carry solar panels if the roof is above the normal level that will be seen from the road and of course assuming that the roof is strong enough and not going to fall down.

Dog kennels will have solar panelling on their roofs to provide heat and light for Fido with any surplus going toward other needs.

Alternative Power Sources

It is time for Ermintrude to make her contribution to the power needs of the country and for her to deposit the vast quantities of methane she gives out in a controlled but painless fashion. For this purpose machines will need to be provided to collect her excess gas at the same time as milking to make the process straightforward and efficient.

There is also the opportunity for some family pets to contribute. There is little point in Hammie or Roland spending his or her day going round inside a wheel that is not connected to some form of generator. They could at the very least be powering the tropical fish tank, although connecting their electrics directly to the water might give rise to some issues. I know of dogs that do actually have a treadmill for indoor exercise and these too could be made better use of.

Chemicals which can affect animals will be banned
The extent to which modern fertilizers and weed killers enter the waterways must be reduced. Many of the chemicals are not good for humans and certainly are not good for other animals either. Although there are restrictions on the proximity to water courses where they can be used, these do not go far enough, as the level of polluted run-off still affects other animals living both above and below ground. There can also be times when the presence of fertilizers, unbeknown to a dog, can cause problems to our paws if we have been walking through the chemicals. I know we could wear boots but isn't it better to stop using chemicals that can do so much harm?

GMO
While we are at it we won't be allowing any genetically modified crops to be grown either, as their impact on the environment has not been proven to be sufficiently safe. You only have to look at how far away from our house there are now purple frilly poppies growing, to realise that the wind takes seeds to other places very effectively and our human hasn't even grown any poppies in the last three years! And don't even get me started on the proliferation of oil seed rape in every hedgerow and on every roadside. It's verging on the ridiculous!

Green future
I'm sure the sunny weather is probably down to global warming and I ought to be jumping up and down and begging you not to create such a big problem, but from

where I am sitting looking out of the window, after chasing round the garden for ages, I can't help but think I rather like it. How do you get people to be concerned about a problem when it seems to be making life better? Maybe some parts of the world are having severe droughts and others may be having worse storms, but sadly, in some of the parts of the world that can probably do most to change things, it is looking pretty good, if you discount the flooding. It is interesting to think about what the canine response to the problem might be. Now I would be the last one to stop people having open fires. There is nothing better than lying on the rug in front of a blazing log fire, and I mean nothing! I don't want to start banning things that I enjoy, but I could put a tax on them. Perhaps a household should be taxed on the emissions from their way of life, based on some complex calculation of fuel usage, number of chimneys, and so on. It could take into account the number of cars they have and the distance travelled, compared of course to the efficiency of the engines. They would then be reduced by the number of trees growing in their gardens. Then the tax people pay could go into planting lots of lovely trees for me to sniff and pee on. Thousands of acres could be turned over to woodland. Inner city sites that are no longer required for development could be turned into miniature woodlands. There could be lines of trees down the central reservations of motorways, which works until they fall down across the road. As I've already said part of the solution is to develop more solar power, but reforestation is definitely an important strategy for us.

The modern trend to smaller gardens with minimal vegetation should be discouraged. There should be special annual incentives for the number of trees someone has in the garden, although there would need to be a maximum number for any area, to give the trees the possibility of growing properly. Come to think of it, the species should be carefully selected to limit the amount of damage to buildings caused by the roots.

WELFARE

Not all dogs that are on the streets are out there because they have got lost. Some are out there because they have fallen on hard times. For some they have been forced out of their homes and for others they have run away to avoid abuse. In fact it seems in places there are whole subcultures of dogs living on the streets, scavenging food and drink and going without home comforts. For some it has become a way of life, not exactly a lifestyle choice but something they have been born into and they know no other way of life. There are organisations which work tirelessly to help the homeless humans, but what about the homeless dogs? Of course there are wonderful charities who do try to help homeless dogs, but they need more support and funding. We will make it our mission to ensure that every dog on the streets is provided with food in the leaner winter months and blankets to snuggle into on cold nights. It shouldn't just be a case of rounding them up and sending them off to a pound, these dogs need help. Some of them may need counselling to help them overcome the difficulties they have faced in life. Some dogs have seen much cruelty and will not readily trust a human. We at the Pet Dogs Democratic Party are committed to work to improve the future of these poor dogs.

Dogs may become homeless when their humans fall on hard times and have their own homes repossessed. It is not uncommon for the homes those families go on to rent to refuse to take pets and when that happens, the animals are cast out or taken to a shelter. It is not acceptable to separate dogs from their families in this way. If humans will not bring in legislation to insist on rental owners not breaking up families then it falls on us to bring in legislation to make it possible for the humans to seek refuge in kennels with their dogs.

This whole 'best friend' thing is only skin deep. When it suits humans to want our faithful companionship then they think that is fine, but on a bad day, there are some humans who see us as just an inconvenience to be disposed of. In order to ensure that humans take their commitments more seriously, in those instances where they abandon their dog, we reserve the right to charge those humans for the upkeep and care of that dog for the rest of that dog's natural life to a minimum of the average age attained by that breed. This would cover any event where a dog died in unfortunate circumstances where the human may have in any way contributed to that death!

The PDDP will campaign for a welfare system to take care of all dogs who fall on hard times. We will set up hospitals and nursing homes for dogs. We will pay benefit to those dogs who can't afford their keep and provide shelters for the homeless. Where we can, we'll team them up with a human being and do a 'two for one' package, give a home to a homeless dog and get a free human thrown in.

ECONOMY AND TAXATION
(BASICALLY MONEY TYPE STUFF)

The expression 'going to the dogs', which is used by humans to mean something is going wrong, should be changed, as it is a complete fallacy. Dogs aren't the ones borrowing much more than they can afford. In fact they don't borrow things at all. They may occasionally take something they weren't meant to have, but they never do this with the intention of either giving it back or paying for the damage. We live within our means.

Initially we need to raise some money, so we will tax all businesses that don't allow access to dogs, an extra 10% on top of current taxes. We will also place a special tax on all households that do not have at least one dog as a household member. Similarly we will tax all car manufacturers that do not fit a dog ramp as standard.

To be honest, it's hard to know how much those measures will raise, so in addition to that there is going to have to be a large reduction in the amount of existing taxes that are spent on humans. We're not sure that education is really appreciated by many children so it should be made optional rather than compulsory, giving them more time to spend at home with their pets.

Tax will be abolished on all dog food and a new Family Pet allowance will be introduced covering all dogs as long as they are provided with indoor sleeping accommodation. We want to see all dogs taken out of the poverty trap and for this we don't mean some

calculation based on averages which means there will always be dogs in poverty. We want this to be an absolute measure. As part of this aim, there will be a one off payment of £500 made to all families giving a home to a dog from a pets' home and this will rise to £750 for those taking in elderly or disabled dogs.

I've thought long and hard about this and despite my misgivings, I am prepared to say that dogs will come under the taxation system. Obviously this will be linked to full employment rights with all wages earned going directly to the dog. This is an opportunity for man's best friend to make a major contribution to the household budget and in these times of recession, that has to be a good thing. He will also have the satisfaction of knowing he is contributing to a better future for the canine population.

Balancing the budget - How do you decide what should go ahead and what shouldn't? You have to remember that everything in place is likely to be important to somebody, otherwise it wouldn't be there in the first place. You can take the easy approach and take things away from those with the weakest voice, at least when they complain you don't hear them. Alternatively, you can take more difficult decision and decide on a qualitative basis (I had to look that one up) what is of most value to society. Of course it is going to concern some people that you delay replacing a country's defence system, but some would argue that that particular defence system wasn't needed in the first place.

There must be money available for parks, as long as they welcome dogs, and for the development of well-lit footpaths for us to walk on safely at night. We want to see the police having greater funding to follow up dog theft more effectively and measures in place to make us safe in our own homes. These are all things which will need funding.

Then you look at the levy being placed on the banks. Now I know this is a popular move and most people suffer at the hands of the banks now and again, but why single them out in particular? Ok, so as yet I don't think any of them offer an account that can be held in the name of a dog, but there are other businesses which make super-profits. Now I'm not saying it's right or wrong. My point is that for every supporter of a change there will be another person who thinks it's unfair. At the end of the day cuts are needed, unless you really think it is ok to live on debt until you are completely bankrupt.

I found it interesting to read that at one point England sold Dunkirk to the French. It made me wonder about the current world economic crisis and whether those countries that couldn't find the money to meet their obligations might like to sell a bit of their country to somewhere else that was not bankrupt. It's a sort of takeover without the war bit. Now you may wonder why a dog would care, but it started me thinking about whether it wasn't the quickest way to get the Pet Dogs Democratic Party into power. All the dogs around the country could raid their piggy banks and club together to buy, for example, Greece. We could then have a whole country run in a manner that is favourable to the dog community. On a more local scale, the same approach could be taken if a local council ran out of money. The council could then sell part of their borough or county to a neighbouring area or even to a private individual, at which point that individual or group could declare independence. (I will return to the question of devotion shortly.)

Puppy Benefit
Now I realise that the size of a litter of puppies will give some grounds for discussion, but I think we need to make the principal of Puppy Benefit clear. It is important that Puppy Benefit is paid direct to the mother to enable her to take care of her puppies effectively and keep them at home for longer. It will be paid until the puppy reaches the age of two and a half years, or longer if the puppy

remains in full time education. If a puppy is sent to live in another home then the benefit for that puppy will cease. It will also cease if the puppy enters full-time paid employment before that age, regardless of whether he is still living at home. It can of course be transferred between the parents if the puppy moves to grow up with his or her father as long as the above conditions are met.

Euro

The Pet Dogs Democratic Party will not be joining the Euro under any circumstances. The Euro is flawed and is bound to fail. It is something to do with individual countries wanting to do what is best for their own economies and for their own people rather than the greater good of Europe. Even if the weakest country were to leave the Euro now, rather than having their economy propped up by other countries, it is inevitable that the problem will be repeated with another country being unable to meet its commitments, and then another. There would be none of this 'widening of the goalposts' to make the game easier. It's a bit like playing musical chairs and not taking a chair out each time because you don't want to upset anyone, even if they are too slow to find a chair.

Besides any economic reasons, where is the romance in all countries having one currency? I get my passport stamped every time I travel. To be fair it is a stamp which says I have been wormed, but I often look back wistfully at the places the vets were from and remember the different journeys I have taken. In the past it was like that for humans too. Their passports were stamped at every border across Europe, the currency changed and confusion set in. Everyone was clueless as to which coin to use or whether a box of dog treats were a bargain or a great expense, but they were the glorious days of travel. Now all we're left with is different languages. How long will it be before that changes and everyone is speaking Spanish or American? ... which thinking about it may become the same thing at some point!

Of course, you may argue that with dogs running the country things would be different and it's a fair point. With the economy in the paws of dogs, the fact that we live life so much more simply would completely change how things work. All we need is the odd biscuit and occasional pat and we're happy. I guess to be fair in a dispute about bones we might just fight it out, but we certainly don't end up with high inflation or a serious balance of payments deficit. I've never taken out a loan and I'm not about to start living on credit now – and that isn't just because I'm not allowed to open a bank account and no one will lend me any money, although to be fair that may be a factor.

TRADE AND INDUSTRY

We will of course be encouraging trade, although it's not an area I know much about yet. We're always willing to learn though. As a dog I really need to know that the energy supply that keeps me warm is not in foreign hands. Therefore what I do know is that we will be encouraging a mix of state run bodies as well as private companies. If we go back to my idea of selling bits of countries to settle debts, there could be all sorts of problems if we don't keep the key assets. Key services which are essential to everyday life will be run by the Government.

That isn't to say that those parts of business and services which are in state hands should not work to commercial standards. Even a dog can see that they should be run on the same basis as the best businesses. However, they will not be required to make a profit to return to shareholders, they will instead be aiming to plough any benefits they achieve back into the business or services they provide. This is certainly how I'd like to see the National Canine Health Service run. I'd like to think we could have as good a standard of treatment as any private patient. Where there are commercial operators in the same field then the Government owned business should aim to achieve the same standards, but will, where appropriate, be subsidised in order to do that.

AGRICULTURE AND FISHING

I've already talked about fertilizers, but in addition to this, pesticides which are harmful to animals will not be allowed. Nor will genetically modified crops. Where possible there will be encouragement to farm organically and the amount of chemical preservatives used on food must be declared on all produce including that sold as 'fresh loose vegetables'. We eat that stuff. We don't want to be eating chemicals. We often have it raw so there is not even the chance of those chemicals having been boiled away. We dogs don't care if our carrots are really orange, but we do care what they taste like and whether they will be good for us.

There will also be a law passed very early in our term of office to prevent waste products, which are not good enough for human consumption, being used in animal food. We deserve to eat food of the highest quality and if you wouldn't eat it, then why should we? Of course there are things which we consider a delicacy that you may want to introduce to the human diet, such as sheep poo and horse manure, but the basic premise is that if it isn't good enough for you then it isn't good enough for us either! Of course you may argue that we have a cast iron constitution compared to humans, but very often that is because we still eat some of those things. Humans keep their lives way too clean and as a result they pay the price.

We're also concerned about the extent to which oil seed rape has taken over the country. No one has thought about the extensive implication to allergy sufferers and nothing is being done to minimise its spreading. Every main road and motorway now seems to be bordered by oil seed rape plants growing wild. It has developed a life of its own. It might look pretty and provide a good fuel alternative, but it is toxic to humans and causes allergic responses in a large number of people and they deserve some consideration.

There needs to be a greater understanding of the important role of the farming community. All school children and puppies should have at least one school trip to stay on or around a working farm. Living in a village, I no longer think that cereal is something that comes out of a packet from the supermarket or that a sheep is something to be chased. I think cereal is something that takes hours of work to grow in the fields and that sheep are to be respected, particularly if the farmer has a gun! When the weather is wet, it doesn't do the crops any good, quite apart from farmers not being able to get the combine harvesters into the waterlogged fields to cut the wheat and having to move sheep to higher ground. Then instead of being able to cut beautiful golden ears of wheat, they are left with dull brown ears that end up as animal feed. This is another example of the maxim that if it isn't good enough for humans, then it isn't good enough for us either. Of course maybe humans shouldn't be quite so fussy, but that's another story.

When I hear the farmers out working until all hours, I can't help but feel grateful for what they do so we can eat. Let's face it, if they weren't doing all the hard work, we'd have to do it ourselves and that is never a good alternative.

Then there is the important question of meat quality.

The checking of meat quality is very important to all of us. Meat entering the food chain should be of the highest quality and I know many dogs who would be happy to work as testers in this area. Admittedly those same dogs are often happy to eat road kill or anything else left lying around, but that isn't to say they couldn't be trained to do a good job.

TRANSPORT

There will be free bus passes for all dogs. It would give us so much more mobility if we could jump onto public transport without having to worry about carrying the right change. It is so difficult, with paws, to count the coins out to buy a ticket. If we could simply hang a bus pass from our collar it would be much easier. Smaller dogs might find it hard to stand up high enough to show the pass to the driver, but for us larger animals, we could simply stand up on our back paws to show or scan our pass.

Roads
Basically roads are a good thing, but there is way too much traffic on them, so it's hard to get anywhere and besides which I don't like the noise. I don't think the answer is to build more roads, that just seems to make the problem worse and apart from that the more there are, the less money there will be to fix the holes in the ones we've got. We need dog walking lanes as well as cycle lanes, to be developed. These need to be much wider than most pavements. In fact they need to be plenty wide enough for us to pull out to the length of an extending lead so we can sniff in safety, without the risk of crossing a cycle lane and catapulting cyclists off their bikes. For reference cyclists don't take being catapulted very well.

We need to get to a point where it is effective to use the railways to transport heavy loads so that there are fewer enormous lorries on the road. We should also be encouraging far more people to work from home. Firstly, it means they can spend time with their beloved dogs and secondly it cuts down on some of the needless travel.

Then there are the road works. You see workmen resurfacing the road in other countries and they seem to have big machines that can do stretches of road much faster. Here we block off miles and miles of road for months on end and simply create more frustration to those who are trying to travel, while apparently making little or no progress with the road. Mind you, where I was born in Belgium, there were frequent 'Omlegging' or diversions as we know them here, but they only ever seemed to take you away from the road you were on and then left you to work it out for yourself! Now, I know we dogs have an inherent sense of direction, particularly where home is concerned, but when we've been sent round several corners and are then asked to find our way without going cross country, or retracing our steps, it's not so easy.

Rail

I may be wrong, but I can't help thinking there should be more trains and ones that stop at more places to make it easy to use them. I know there used to be stations in all sorts of places and I really can't understand why they aren't there anymore. It would be so much easier to get around if there were local trains and ones that ran on a regular basis. It would also help if you knew you would be able to get a seat, or in my case enough room to sit down without having my paws and tail trodden on.

It may be that the trains need to be managed centrally to make it all possible or they should at least receive subsidies so that they can afford to run services to rural areas. I don't think we should be putting in lots of new expensive lines going to the places that already have good services, we should be spending the money making it possible to get to more places and opening up the old rail network. In some places it will mean putting some track back down, but that has to be easier than starting from scratch. Just think how happy it would make thousands of train spotters. From a dog's point of view it is also much better to have our human free to play with us and give us some attention while we're travelling. It's not fun when they are driving and have to stay focussed on the road ahead, particularly when they refuse to play I-spy. Rail and bus travel are definitely the way forward for accompanied dogs, unless we can get car manufacturers to make enough modifications to cars to enable us to drive them effectively and safely.

There is then the matter of how much a dog is charged to travel. Now, generally it seems to be that we are charged half fare, the same as children. That seems fair enough until you think about the fact that they are allowed to sit on the seats and we are expected to sit on the floor. We don't take up any more space than they do, unless by 'we' I am referring to Great Danes and Irish Wolfhounds, in which case half price seems like a bargain. I am about the weight of a medium sized child and I can sit very nicely and be quiet, unlike most medium sized children. If I am going to have to pay half fare I think I should be entitled to a seat. Otherwise I should be paying less. The floor is not a privilege.

Busses

In principal I think busses are a good idea. In practice I prefer trams as they are smoother and more comfortable. It's a shame that installing trams is so expensive and such a big job, but maybe it would be good to have more of them in towns where they can fit.

All public transport should give greater consideration to where dogs can sit. There should be areas with little blankets so we don't have to sit on the floor. Have you seen some of the rubbish and dirt down there and I don't even want to mention the things we see stuck under seats.

Public transport should have those anti-bacterial paw cleaning dispensers like the ones in hospitals, to reduce the risk of the spread of disease. It comes to something when it's the dog being concerned about levels of dirt!

ANIMAL TESTING

Europe has already banned the testing of cosmetics on dogs. Which is fair, as how many dogs have you seen actually wearing make-up? When you've got eyes as gorgeous as mine, who needs mascara or eye liner? I will confess that I am looking forward to the benefits of hair care products as I get older, to cover up the grey bits, but that's as far as the vanity goes.

The approach of the PDDP would be a little different from this blanket ban and would extend to all experimentation on dogs. We will make it illegal to carry out any experiment on dogs without their written consent.

I am all in favour of the advancement of science, but a dog should be given a free choice as to whether he is involved in such programmes and paid a good rate of pay, linked to the level of danger which is involved in the work. Take smoking for example. How many Beagles now have a 20 a day habit? How are they supposed to fund that habit when the research programme throws them out? It's an important consideration. You see Beagles hanging round street corners with their paws shaking through the withdrawal symptoms. They are standing there with a hacking cough and it's a giveaway that they used to work in scientific research. It's not a good way to end your days.

With regards to make up and perfume testing, let's be reasonable, you'd have poodles queuing up if you advertised vacancies in those areas, but for the rest of us it really isn't the sort of job for a self-respecting dog. Food testing I might be prepared to try, but it should be my free choice. No dog should be involved in any form of research without signing a form to say he is there of his own free will. He should also be able to leave whenever he chooses, be paid well and have free medical care available for the rest of his life. There should also be compensation to his family if that life is shorter than it would otherwise have been.

We will extend the legislation preventing selling cigarettes to humans under the age of 18 to include dogs under two and half years of age, although I don't suppose many buy their own.

DISABILITY / DIFFERING ABILITY

The PDDP will introduce legislation for every car to have a built in dog ramp.

I've been thinking about disabled dogs and how they

are best cared for. Obviously we prefer to see them looked after in their own homes and able to lead as normal a life as possible. There should be provision made for all their support needs. I'm thinking that dogs could have a lot of fun with motorised transport and that 'dog cart' racing could take on a whole new meaning if the carts had motors and we got to do the driving. Maybe it shouldn't just be disabled dogs that benefit from these improvements. I quite fancy a little motorised cart of my own. I think we should probably draw the line at them falling into the paws of blind dogs, unless they are accompanied by a seeing companion that knows his left paw from his right paw!

CHURCH

The role of the State in the church is not viewed in quite the same light by dogs. As we don't marry, the question of divorce is irrelevant! We are not included in most religions and seem to get by perfectly well. We object to being seen as 'dirty' by some and an irrelevance by others. You have your Heaven, we have our Rainbow Bridge. If anything is created in the image of God then surely it is dog, the reverse image. We aren't going to interfere; on the whole we see the value of a moral code to live by as long as it is applied in our interests. We are thinking of making some minor alterations to some of the wording of hymns however.

I have been reading through a few Christmas carols and am a little put out that the Shepherds always seem to get a mention, but not the sheepdogs. Where would the shepherds have been without their dogs? Who do you think was left minding the flocks so they could go and take a look at what the star was all about? Christmas carols should be less discriminatory. Christmas should be a time of inclusion. Firstly we would like While Shepherds Watched to read as follows:

While sheepdogs watched their flocks by night
All lying on the ground
The angel of the Lord came down
And glory shone around.
"Bark not," said he for there they were

PET DOGS DEMOCRATIC PARTY MANIFESTO

All woofs and other sounds
"Glad tidings of great joy I bring
To you and other hounds."

I've also looked a rather more secular version of God Rest Ye Merry Gentlemen, to be sung as follows:

God speed ye resting carting dogs
Let nothing you dismay
For Santa's reindeer want a rest
You need to pull his sleigh
To take the presents round the world
In time for Christmas Day

Look lively now there's a good boy
there's a good boy
Look lively now there's a good boy.

PARLIAMENT

Cleaning Up Politics
There is the important matter of MPs expenses. I have reached the opinion that, for us, paying for a second home would be a modest affair and even if you threw in a lifetime's supply of dog biscuits it would be hard to spend as much as one human MP has spent on horse manure. Furthermore, while we might find the peculiar tang of horse manure quite inviting, it is not something we would pay for. We generally find sheep, fox or even cat poo a good substitute for our needs and I'm sure some of the MP in question's neighbours would be happy to furnish him with spare cat poo to put on his garden.

As a dog, I can assure voters that my expenses would be limited. I suppose I might pick up one or two kennel fees when travelling, but nothing of any consequence.

Bribery is basically a bad thing. The good news is that dogs are generally not driven by money. Every effort would be made to resist bribery by biscuits, although I can't promise that we couldn't be bought for a small piece of finest steak.

Parliamentary structure
The House of Lords in its current format would be replaced by a body of appointed individuals who would serve for no more than 10 years. They would be selected by a random computer programme to reflect a cross section of British society, with members drawn from all

walks of life including household pets.

The position would be a paid appointment, paying the same level as the person or pet was earning in the outside world and would increase each year by the rate of inflation. For those not earning at the point of appointment they would be paid at a basic minimum figure. They would receive a year's pay on completion of their term to allow for transition back into their normal life. Anyone between the human equivalent ages of 18 and 80 could be eligible for inclusion. If they declined then the next person would be selected and if they resigned during office they would not be entitled to their additional year's pay. Of course with the household pets, if there were any unfortunate incidents of one eating another (a mouse by a cat for example) a pension would be paid to the family of the deceased animal and the offender would be fired from the position for 'gross misconduct' without further payment being made. Legal proceedings may also be taken against the offending animal.

To avoid them all having to be based in London there could be regional premises linked by video conference to enable debate to continue.

To be honest, it might not work awfully well but it could be fun trying. Although, there may be certain restrictions on what can count as a 'household pet' for the purpose of being selected. Pythons, tarantulas, cockroaches and performing ants need not apply.

Devolution

While we are on the subject of regional assemblies it is right to say something about devolution. The question of whether the Scots were right or wrong is a moot point. Where was Greyfriars Bobbie in all the hype or discussion? Or, more to the point, where were his descendants? Why did you not see a long line of West Highland Terriers going to the polls, or Gordon Setters invited to take part in the debates?

Some of the points the Scottish politicians made were valid for all the countries within the United Kingdom. London can seem a very long way away, not only geographically, but also culturally if you are living in a rural area hundreds of miles from Westminster. To be honest it probably seems culturally distant if you are a young terrier living in the East End of London, never mind as a Bearded Collie in the lowlands of Scotland. The pomp and ceremony of Parliament might be a great part of our culture and a good way to attract tourists, but is it any wonder that the average 18 year old feels it has little relevance to their life?

Quite apart from all that, what is wrong with being English, Scottish, Welsh and Northern Irish and still working together within the United Kingdom. It is frowned upon to state your nationality as anything beyond British (which obviously does not include Northern Ireland). My human always puts English or England on forms, as that is what she is and that is where she is from. She is still happy for England to be part of Great Britain and for Great Britain to be part of the United Kingdom, but why should the actual country be forgotten in all that? You probably think that as a Swiss breed born in the Flemish part of Belgium I don't have a right to comment on all this, but when has that stopped me?

Anyway, we will introduce regional assemblies to deal with all issues that do not need to be dealt with at a 'national' level. Obviously foreign policy, defence and some aspects of the economy such as those impacting the currency need to be managed at one central level, but there is no reason that everything else can't be done regionally with for these purposes Scotland, Wales and Northern Ireland being deemed regions (although I do know they are countries). England could be covered as one region or as several, the latter being more appropriate given the size of the population. Each of those assemblies could then be represented in the national parliament. Not only will this make it easier for dogs to attend sittings of the assemblies but it will also make it easier for the humans who are part of it to get home to their beloved pets each evening.

Fixed Term Parliaments

As it is now, Parliaments will be for a fixed five year term without the opportunity for anyone to manipulate the election date for when they are more popular. The Upper Chamber will have an appointment date at the mid-point of a Parliamentary term so they never all change at once.

We reserve the right to change this policy in the event that we are elected to Parliament with a majority and decide we'd quite like to stay in power a little longer.

Our Nations Flag

Lastly and no less importantly, there will be a redesign of our British flag to incorporate man's best friend. I understand it will make it even harder for school children to draw, but it's bad enough already and very few people know which way up it goes. Anyway, it is important to reflect our improved status and the special relationship we should enjoy in a 'nation of dog lovers'. I will concede the picture might have to be a Corgi, in honour of the wishes of our monarch, but that could always be voted on in a referendum – a sort of cutest puppy competition on a much bigger scale.

HOUSING AND PLANNING

Of course I realise we need a policy on housing, but we are so much less demanding than humans in this regard. We don't need a kitchen as our food normally comes prepared; Although we love it when you drop food on the kitchen floor while you are preparing your own dinner. We don't by choice need a bathroom, in the sense of a bath, although we would like an inside toilet for use in bad weather and in emergencies. What we really want is adequate shelter from the elements, preferably with an open fire to sit near when we're cold and a nice stone floor to lie on when we get too hot. A comfy bed and a settee for variety are always appreciated. We don't need 'spare bedrooms' or 'en-suite bathrooms' or 'wine cellars' or 'lofts'. It doesn't have to be large. If we feel hemmed in, we just go outside. At a push we'll even sleep in a pile so we can fit more of us into a small space. What we want most of all is human company, a special someone to share our small space with. If only it were as simple as that when it came to humans. Just think how easy it would be to address the housing shortage if we all looked at it that way. We wouldn't have the levels of house inflation in some areas either, as on the whole we'll live just about anywhere and have no desire to be in or near big cities. Nor, frankly, do we care about the value of our property or worry about whether it is in the 'right' area. Once we've got past safe and well fed our demands are fairly limited.

I should at this point however say that dogs should only sleep in kennels by choice and not compulsion. It should be a little like a human going 'glamping' one step up from a tent, but not something you would do every day, unless you're really weird. I do realise there are dogs who would choose to do it every day, in the same way there are humans who think that living like that is a lifestyle choice, but I will never understand them. I do understand that long haired dogs often find the overheated houses of humans are too warm and do prefer an outdoor sleeping arrangement. For my part, despite being a mountain dog, I have gone a little soft and would not dream of making that choice.

We will not allow building on Green Field Sites, however well you know the Prime Minister or are prepared to pass us a large bag of dog treats. The countryside will be protected from the creeping development that has been allowed to take place. Our rabbit chasing meadows will be safe from the bulldozer. England's 'green and pleasant land' (as well as Scotland's, Wales's and Northern Ireland's) will be just that – green and pleasant, not covered with new housing developments. Redevelopment of disused and derelict premises will be encouraged to improve those areas while protecting the rural landscape. Where is a dog to run carefree if the land is all given over to housing or industrialisation? Where is he to enjoy a meander through woods or chase butterflies across fields if they have been sacrificed to development?

EUROPE

The Pet Dogs Democratic Party believes in the concept of a Europe without frontiers. Sadly, at present this status seems to be a myth. I drove over the border from Belgium to France the other day. If the whole EU thing is working as intended, apart from the odd welcome sign you shouldn't be able to notice a difference. Of course, there are different speed limits, road signs and number plates. Then there is the language difference. These however are nothing to the fact there were actually customs officials slowing everyone down and stopping some cars as they crossed the border. This makes it seem just a tiny bit unreasonable that over the years everyone has pointed the finger at the United Kingdom for retaining border control in both passports and customs. I don't know what the French are concerned will be entering their country from Belgium, we are a pretty innocent bunch. Perhaps they are worried about people 'importing' better chocolate! I know they have put border controls in place between France and Italy because they are upset about their citizens going over the border to buy cheaper cigarettes in Italy. This is somewhat ironic as they have been happy to encourage all the English day-trippers to go to France to buy cheaper cigarettes there for many years.

Our party will insist that European policies are implemented to the same extent in all member states. Whether that means life in the UK will become a little more relaxed and we can give up on trying so hard, or whether it means that the black markets in other countries will reduce and everything becomes more tightly regulated, remains to be decided. No longer will one country be expected to take things seriously if no one else is.

CONCLUSION

At this important stage in our Country's history it is time to vote for a more equal society, a more just society. It is time to vote for a society in which two-legs and four-legs stand together; where mutual trust and respect engender a wholly new way of working for the common good. It is time to vote for a society in which man and dog work in partnership for a better future for us all. A vote for the Pet Dogs Democratic Party is a vote for your best friend, a vote for the most loyal companion you will ever have and who wants what's best for dog and man together. Vote PDDP.

AUTHOR PROFILES

Alfie Dog

Alfie Dog is an Entlebucher Mountain Dog. He was born in Belgium in 2005 and his full name is Einstein van de Tiendenschuur. Although he lived in Belgium for the first two years of his life he moved to the United Kingdom in 2008 and has lived in North Yorkshire ever since. He is widely travelled around Western Europe and has visited France, the Netherlands, Luxembourg and Switzerland as well of course as Belgium. He started writing his diary at the age of 10 weeks and, with the exception of the odd day, when his human was in hospital and he couldn't find the password, he has written it every day since. You can find his diary at www.alfiedog.me.uk He is also the author of the novel 'Alfie's Woods', which he co-wrote with his human and which is based on the lovely woods he enjoyed as a puppy, combined with a vivid imagination of a money laundering hedgehog who had escaped from the Woodland Prison.

He lives with Shadow (Aisha Princess of Beauty) who, at the time of writing, is mother to 18 of the 50 Entlebuchers in the UK and due to have her final litter this year. His other companion is Aristotle, Shadow's wayward son, who terrorises Alfie whilst idolising him at the same time.

Rosemary J. Kind

Rosemary J. Kind is quite clearly mad. She has now co-authored two books with her dog and assists him with the technology for writing his diary. She is the only person we know who has called her business after her dog, and she is utterly devoted to developing the Entlebucher Mountain Dog breed in the UK, having first come across it in 1998 in the Encyclopaedia of Dogs.

She has published five books in her own right including one non-fiction book 'Negotiation Skills for Lawyers', one book of poetry 'Poems for Life', two novels 'The Appearance of Truth' and 'The Lifetracer' and a humorous look at travelling on the London Underground 'Lovers Take up Less Space'. She lives in North Yorkshire with her long-suffering husband and three dogs.

OTHER BOOKS BY THE AUTHORS

Alfie's Diary – Alfie Dog with a little help from Rosemary J. Kind

Alfie Dog, the champion of the rights of the underdog, brings you 'Alfie's Diary – Dog enough not to be human, human enough to be a pet.' Alfie has written his diary as an internet blog since the age of 10 weeks old, developing a growing, loyal reader base and has now pulled together the best of the first year of his diary in book form. His diary presents an entertaining and thought provoking dog's eye view of the world.

Alfie's Woods – Alfie Dog with a little help from Rosemary J. Kind

Alfie is fascinated when Hedgehog is recaptured following his escape from the Woodland Prison. Too young to understand money laundering, Alfie assumes that Hedgehog should be given sympathy for washing his money. Hedgehog, overwhelmed that any other creature should care about him, finds the strength to change his life. As an ex-convict Hedgehog meets with opposition at every step and it is only the faith of his friends and their unwavering support that enables him to turn his life round. Alfie's Woods is a story of the power of friendship and the difference it can make to all of us.

The Appearance of Truth – Rosemary J. Kind

Lisa Forster begins to trace her family tree. She very quickly discovers that the birth certificate she has had for thirty years is for a baby who died at the age of four months old and is not in fact her own. Her apparently happy middle class upbringing is a myth and her parents had a dark secret. With Pete Laundon's help Lisa sets about discovering the truth. Assuming she is adopted she follows up all possible routes, until with no options left she goes to the newspaper for help. After 30 years, who if anyone knows the truth?

The Lifetracer – Rosemary J. Kind

When Connor Bancroft is asked to investigate a death threat, sent on a countdown clock, he is unwittingly drawn into a complex story of revenge. He uncovers a series of murders, apparently linked only by the clock left with the victim. Connor is more used to dealing with infidelity than murder and is nowhere close to solving the crimes. Now, his eight year old son, Mikey's life is in danger and Connor has little time left to find out – Who is The Lifetracer?

Lovers Take up Less Space – Rosemary J. Kind

Lovers Take up Less Space is a humorous review of the addictive misery of commuting on London Underground. A blow by blow account of everything from how to find breathing space on a packed Tube train, to the psychological torture of your fellow passengers eating a fresh hot bag of chips and not passing them round. It includes games to transform underground travel from a necessary evil to a spare time recreational activity, together with surprising facts and figures answering questions you had not yet thought to ask. Not for the faint hearted. This book will open your eyes to experiences your senses have long since ignored in the interest of sanity.

Alfie Dog Fiction

Taking your imagination for a walk

www.alfiedog.com

Join us on Facebook
http://www.facebook.com/AlfieDogLimited

www.ingramcontent.com/pod-product-compliance
Lightning Source LLC
Chambersburg PA
CBHW071520040426
42444CB00008B/1730